P9-BZP-483

Full Color on Every Page!

America Online®
Simplified® 3rd Edition

**Covers
America Online
Version 7.0**

Visual™

From
maranGraphics®

&

Hungry Minds™

Best-Selling Books • Digital Downloads • e-books • Answer Networks •
e-Newsletters • Branded Web Sites • e-learning

New York, NY ♦ Cleveland, OH ♦ Indianapolis, IN

America Online® Simplified, 3rd Edition

Published by
Hungry Minds, Inc.
909 Third Avenue
New York, NY 10022
www.hungryminds.com

Copyright© 2002 by maranGraphics Inc.
5755 Coopers Avenue
Mississauga, Ontario, Canada
L4Z 1R9

Library of Congress Control Number: 2002100392
ISBN: 0-7645-3673-7
Printed in the United States of America
10 9 8 7 6 5 4 3 2 1
1K/SR/QV/QS/MG

Distributed in the United States by Hungry Minds, Inc.
Distributed by CDG Books Canada Inc. for Canada; by Transworld Publishers Limited in the United Kingdom; by IDG Norge Books for Norway; by IDG Sweden Books for Sweden; by IDG Books Australia Publishing Corporation Pty. Ltd. for Australia and New Zealand; by TransQuest Publishers Pte Ltd. for Singapore, Malaysia, Thailand, Indonesia, and Hong Kong; by Gotop Information Inc. for Taiwan; by ICG Muse, Inc. for Japan; by Intersoft for South Africa; by Eyrolles for France; by International Thomson Publishing for Germany, Austria and Switzerland; by Distribuidora Cuspide for Argentina; by LR International for Brazil; by Galileo Libros for Chile; by Ediciones ZETA S.C.R. Ltda. for Peru; by WS Computer Publishing Corporation, Inc. for the Philippines; by Contemporanea de Ediciones for Venezuela; by Express Computer Distributors for the Caribbean and West Indies; by Micronesia Media Distributor, Inc. for Micronesia; by Chips Computadoras S.A. de C.V. for Mexico; by Editorial Norma de Panama S.A. for Panama; by American Bookshops for Finland.
For corporate orders, please call maranGraphics at 800-469-6616 or fax 905-890-9434.
For general information on Hungry Minds' products and services, please contact our Customer Care Department within the U.S. at 800-762-2974, outside the U.S. at 317-572-3993 or fax 317-572-4002.
For sales inquiries and reseller information, including discounts, premium and bulk quantity sales, and foreign-language translations, please contact our Customer Care Department at 800-434-3422, fax 317-572-4002, or write to Hungry Minds, Inc., Attn: Customer Care Department, 10475 Crosspoint Boulevard, Indianapolis, IN 46256.
For information on licensing foreign or domestic rights, please contact our Sub-Rights Customer Care Department at 212-844-5000.
For information on using Hungry Minds' products and services in the classroom or for ordering examination copies, please contact our Educational Sales Department at 800-434-2086 or fax 317-572-4005.
For press review copies, author interviews, or other publicity information, please contact our Public Relations department at 317-572-3168 or fax 317-572-4168.
For authorization to photocopy items for corporate, personal, or educational use, please contact maranGraphics at the address above.

Trademark Acknowledgments

Permissions

 is a trademark of Hungry Minds, Inc.

U.S. Corporate Sales	**U.S. Trade Sales**
Contact maranGraphics at (800) 469-6616 or fax (905) 890-9434.	Contact Hungry Minds at (800) 434-3422 or fax (317) 572-4002.

Some comments from our readers...

"Compliments To The Chef!! Your books are extraordinary! Or, simply put, Extra-Ordinary, meaning way above the rest! THANK YOU THANK YOU THANK YOU! for creating these. I buy them for friends, family, and colleagues."

    – *Christine J. Manfrin (Castle Rock, CO)*

"What fantastic teaching books you have produced! Congratulations to you and your staff. You deserve the Nobel prize in Education in the Software category. Thanks for helping me to understand computers."

    – *Bruno Tonon (Melbourne, Australia)*

"I was introduced to maranGraphics about four years ago and YOU ARE THE GREATEST THING THAT EVER HAPPENED TO INTRODUCTORY COMPUTER BOOKS!"

    – *Glenn Nettleton (Huntsville, AL)*

"I'm a grandma who was pushed by an 11-year-old grandson to join the computer age. I found myself hopelessly confused and frustrated until I discovered the Visual series. I'm no expert by any means now, but I'm a lot further along than I would have been otherwise. Thank you!"

    – *Carol Louthain (Logansport, IN)*

"Thank you, thank you, thank you...for making it so easy for me to break into this high-tech world. I now own four of your books. I recommend them to anyone who is a beginner like myself. Now...if you could just do one for programming VCRs, it would make my day!"

    – *Gay O'Donnell (Calgary, Alberta, Canada)*

"I write to extend my thanks and appreciation for your books. They are clear, easy to follow, and straight to the point. Keep up the good work!"

    – *Seward Kollie (Dakar, Senegal)*

"Thank you for making it a lot easier to learn the basics."

    – *Allan Black (Woodlawn, Ontario, Canada)*

"Your books are superior! An avid reader since childhood, I've consumed literally tens of thousands of books, a significant quantity in the learning/teaching category. Your series is the most precise, visually appealing, and compelling to peruse. Kudos!"

    – *Margaret Chmilar (Edmonton, Alberta, Canada)*

"I just want to tell you how much I, a true beginner, really enjoy your books and now understand a lot more about my computer and working with Windows. I'm 51 and a long time out of the classroom, but these books make it easier for me to learn. Hats off to you for a great product."

    – *William K. Rodgers (Spencer, NC)*

"I would like to take this time to thank you and your company for producing great and easy to learn products. I bought two of your books from a local bookstore, and it was the best investment I've ever made!"

    – *Jeff Eastman (West Des Moines, IA)*

"I would like to take this time to compliment maranGraphics on creating such great books. Thank you for making it clear. Keep up the good work."

    – *Kirk Santoro (Burbank, CA)*

"I have to praise you and your company on the fine products you turn out. Thank you for creating books that are easy to follow. Keep turning out those quality books."

    – *Gordon Justin (Brielle, NJ)*

"Over time, I have bought a number of your 'Read Less-Learn More' books. For me, they are THE way to learn anything easily. I learn easiest using your method of teaching."

    – *José A. Mazón (Cuba, NY)*

maranGraphics is a family-run business located near Toronto, Canada.

At **maranGraphics**, we believe in producing great computer books—one book at a time.

Each maranGraphics book uses the award-winning communication process that we have been developing over the last 25 years. Using this process, we organize screen shots, text and illustrations in a way that makes it easy for you to learn new concepts and tasks.

We spend hours deciding the best way to perform each task, so you don't have to! Our clear, easy-to-follow screen shots and instructions walk you through each task from beginning to end.

Our detailed illustrations go hand-in-hand with the text to help reinforce the information. Each illustration is a labor of love—some take up to a week to draw!

We want to thank you for purchasing what we feel are the best computer books money can buy. We hope you enjoy using this book as much as we enjoyed creating it!

Sincerely,

The Maran Family

Please visit us on the Web at:

www.maran.com

Credits

Author:
Ruth Maran

Copy Development Directors:
Wanda Lawrie
Cathy Lo

Project Manager:
Judy Maran

Editors:
Roderick Anatalio
Norm Schumacher
Megan Kirby

**Layout Designer
and Illustrator:**
Treena Lees

Illustrators:
Russ Marini
Steven Schaerer

**Screen Artist
and Illustrator:**
Darryl Grossi

**Illustration Review and
Screen Permissions:**
Roxanne Van Damme

Indexer:
Cathy Lo

**Senior Vice President
and Publisher, Hungry Minds
Technology Publishing Group:**
Richard Swadley

**Publishing Director,
Hungry Minds Technology
Publishing Group:**
Barry Pruett

**Editorial Support,
Hungry Minds Technology
Publishing Group:**
Jennifer Dorsey
Sandy Rodrigues
Lindsay Sandman

Post Production:
Robert Maran

Acknowledgments

Thanks to the dedicated staff of maranGraphics, including
Roderick Anatalio, Darryl Grossi, Kelleigh Johnson,
Megan Kirby, Wanda Lawrie, Treena Lees,
Cathy Lo, Jill Maran, Judy Maran, Robert Maran,
Ruth Maran, Russ Marini, Steven Schaerer,
Norm Schumacher, Raquel Scott, Roxanne Van Damme
and Paul Whitehead.

Finally, to Richard Maran who originated the easy-to-use
graphic format of this guide. Thank you for your
inspiration and guidance.

Table of Contents

Table of Contents

CHAPTER 7

CHAT WITH AOL MEMBERS

CHAPTER 8

ATTEND LIVE EVENTS

CHAPTER 9

USING MESSAGE BOARDS

CHAPTER 10

CREATE AND JOIN GROUPS

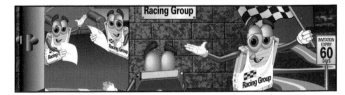

CHAPTER 11

CUSTOMIZE AOL

CHAPTER 12

WORK WITH PASSWORDS AND SCREEN NAMES

CHAPTER 13

COOL AOL FEATURES

CHAPTER 1

GETTING STARTED

Are you ready to begin using AOL? This chapter will provide you with the basics you need to get started.

America Online (AOL) is a graphical, easy-to-use online service that offers a wide range of information and features.

Founded in 1985, AOL now has more than 33 million members.

Obtain the AOL Software

You need to install the AOL software to access AOL. You can obtain the software and a free trial membership by calling 1-800-827-6364. If you have access to the Internet, you can download the software from the www.aol.com/try Web site.

Connect to AOL

Most people use a modem to connect to AOL. A modem transmits information over telephone lines. AOL also supports high-speed connections. A high-speed connection transfers information faster than a modem connection and allows you to keep your telephone line free while connected to AOL. AOL provides some specialized content that is available only to members with high-speed connections.

Screen Name

When you set up an account on AOL, you must choose a screen name. A screen name identifies each person on AOL. You can create up to seven screen names to allow your family members and friends to use your AOL account.

WHAT YOU CAN DO ON AOL

Obtain Information

AOL offers an enormous amount of information that is organized into channels such as Entertainment, News and Travel. You can quickly find information of interest on AOL by using keywords such as **Movies** and **Weather**.

You can also use AOL to access the vast amount of information available on the World Wide Web.

Exchange Electronic Mail

You can exchange electronic mail (e-mail) with AOL members and people on the Internet. E-mail provides a fast, economical and convenient way to send messages to family members, friends and colleagues.

Use the Buddy List

You can use the Buddy List to see when your friends, family members and colleagues are online and send them instant messages. An instant message you send will immediately appear on the other person's screen.

Chat With AOL Members and Attend Live Events

You can have online conversations with other AOL members. Chatting is a great way to ask questions and exchange ideas with other members. AOL also offers live, interactive events where you can exchange questions and comments with special guests, including athletes, movie stars, politicians and writers.

Use Message Boards and Groups

AOL offers message boards you can use to exchange information with AOL members who share your interests. You can also create a group on AOL to discuss a specific topic with other AOL members.

Cool AOL Features

➢ You can use Radio@AOL to listen to music stations on AOL.

➢ AOL offers thousands of files, such as images, sounds, games and programs, that you can download and then use on your computer.

➢ You can have a roll of film developed and then sent to your AOL account so you can share the pictures with friends and family members. You can also store pictures you took with a digital camera on your AOL account.

You can connect to AOL at any time to access the information and features AOL offers.

If your computer can play sound, you will hear "Welcome" when you connect to AOL. If you have new e-mail messages, you will also hear "You've Got Mail."

CONNECT TO AOL

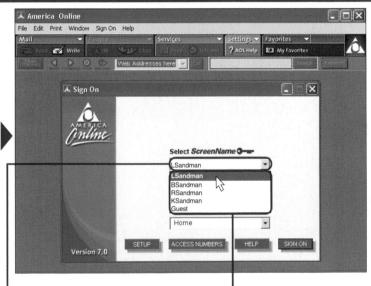

1 Double-click the America Online icon on your desktop.

■ The America Online window and the Sign On window appear.

2 Click this area to display a list of the screen names set up on your AOL account. A screen name identifies each person on AOL.

3 Click the screen name you want to use to connect to AOL.

Why did this dialog box appear when I tried to connect to AOL?

The first time you use your screen name to connect to AOL, this dialog box appears, allowing you to store your password. Storing your password saves you from having to type the password each time you connect to AOL.

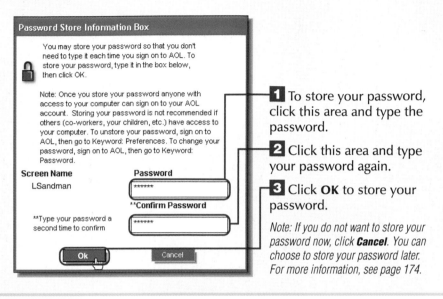

1 To store your password, click this area and type the password.

2 Click this area and type your password again.

3 Click **OK** to store your password.

*Note: If you do not want to store your password now, click **Cancel**. You can choose to store your password later. For more information, see page 174.*

4 Click this area and type the password for your screen name. An asterisk (*) appears for each character you type to prevent others from seeing your password.

*Note: If an area does not appear for you to type your password, the password is stored. Skip to step **5**. For information about storing your password, see the top of this page.*

5 Click **Sign On** to connect to AOL.

■ The Welcome window appears each time you connect to AOL. Other windows may also appear.

■ This area displays information specific to your city, such as the weather and local news headlines.

EXIT AOL

1 Click ⊠ to exit AOL.

■ If your computer can play sound, you will hear "Goodbye."

The America Online window displays many items that help you access information and use the features AOL offers.

Menu Bar

Provides access to lists of commands available in AOL.

Toolbar

Contains menus that provide access to AOL features, such as Live Events and Parental Controls. The toolbar also contains buttons you can select to quickly access commonly used features, such as Chat and My Favorites.

Navigation Bar

Contains controls you can use when browsing through information on the World Wide Web.

Welcome Window

The Welcome window appears each time you connect to AOL. This window displays content specific to your city, such as the weather and local news headlines, and provides quick access to information and features offered by AOL.

SCROLL THROUGH A WINDOW

You can use a scroll bar to browse through the information in a window. Scrolling is useful when a window is not large enough to display all the information it contains.

SCROLL THROUGH A WINDOW

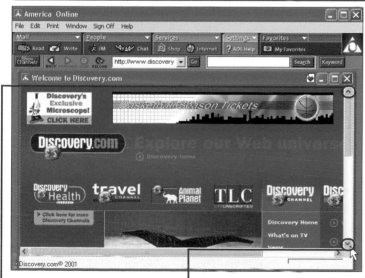

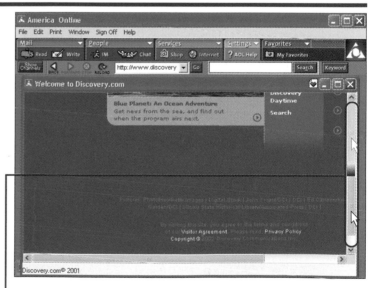

SCROLL UP

1 Click ⌃ to scroll up through the information in a window.

SCROLL DOWN

1 Click ⌄ to scroll down through the information in a window.

SCROLL TO ANY POSITION

1 Position the mouse over the scroll box.

2 Drag the scroll box along the scroll bar until the information you want to view appears.

■ The location of the scroll box indicates which part of the window you are viewing. For example, when the scroll box is halfway down the scroll bar, you are viewing information from the middle of the window.

You can maximize a window to fill your screen. This allows you to view more of the window's contents.

MAXIMIZE A WINDOW

1 Click 🗖 in the window you want to maximize.

Note: If the 🗖 button is dimmed, you cannot maximize the window.

■ The window fills your screen.

■ To return the window to its previous size, click 🗗.

■ You can also double-click the title bar of a window to maximize the window.

MINIMIZE A WINDOW

If you are not using a window, you can minimize the window to temporarily remove it from your screen. You can redisplay the window at any time.

Minimizing a window allows you to temporarily put a window aside so you can work on other tasks.

MINIMIZE A WINDOW

1 Click ▬ in the window you want to minimize.

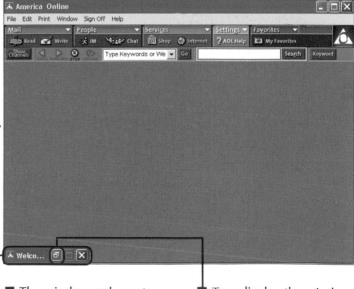

■ The window reduces to a bar at the bottom of your screen.

■ To redisplay the window, click 🗗 .

MOVE A WINDOW

If a window covers items on your screen, you can move the window to a different location.

You may want to move several windows to see the contents of multiple windows at once.

MOVE A WINDOW

1 Position the mouse over the title bar of the window you want to move.

2 Drag the mouse to where you want to place the window.

Note: You cannot move a window over the navigation bar or toolbar.

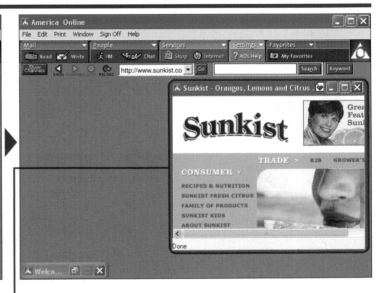

■ The window moves to the new location.

Note: You cannot move a maximized window. For information about maximizing a window, see page 10.

RESIZE A WINDOW

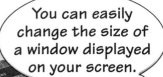

You can easily change the size of a window displayed on your screen.

Enlarging the size of a window allows you to view more information in the window. Reducing the size of a window allows you to view items covered by the window.

RESIZE A WINDOW

1 Position the mouse ⬚ over an edge of the window you want to resize (⬚ changes to ↔, ↕, ⤢ or ⤡).

Note: You cannot resize some windows.

2 Drag the mouse ↔ until the window displays the size you want.

■ The window displays the new size.

Note: You cannot resize a maximized window. For information about maximizing a window, see page 10.

When you finish working with a window, you can close the window to remove it from your screen.

CLOSE A WINDOW

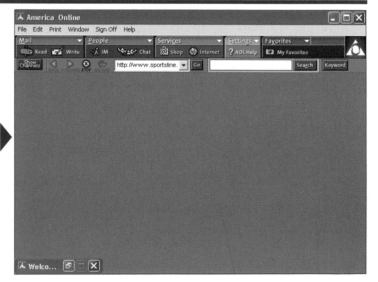

1 Click ✕ in the window you want to close.

Note: You cannot close the Welcome window. When you click the ✕ button in the Welcome window, the window reduces to a bar at the bottom of your screen. For more information about minimizing a window, see page 11.

■ The window disappears from your screen.

SWITCH BETWEEN WINDOWS

If you have more than one window open on your screen, you can easily switch between the windows.

You can work in only one window at a time. The active window appears in front of all other windows and displays a dark title bar.

SWITCH BETWEEN WINDOWS

1 To display a list of all open windows, click **Window**.

2 Click the name of the window you want to display.

■ A check mark (✔) indicates which window currently appears in front of all other windows.

■ The window appears in front of all other windows. You can now clearly view the contents of the window.

Note: You can also click anywhere inside a window to display the window in front of all other windows.

15

SEARCH FOR HELP INFORMATION

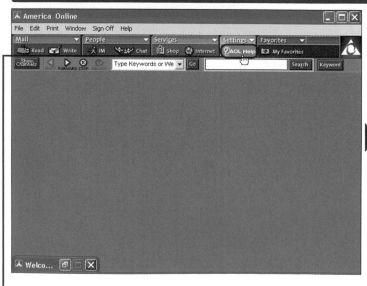

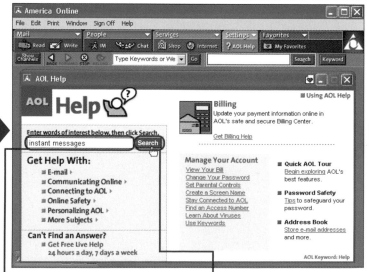

1 Click **AOL Help**.

■ The AOL Help window appears.

2 Click this area and type a word or phrase that describes the task you want help with.

3 Click **Search** to start the search.

■ The AOL Help Search Results for window appears.

When viewing a help article, why do some words appear underlined and blue in color?

Words that appear underlined and blue in color are links that will display AOL areas related to the help article you are currently viewing. To display a related AOL area, click the underlined word.

Is there another way I can get help information?

Many AOL windows display a Help button. You can click this button to view help information about a task you want to perform in the window.

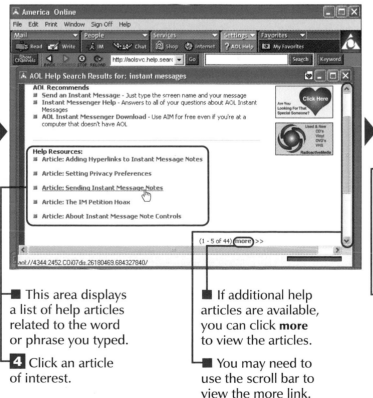

■ This area displays a list of help articles related to the word or phrase you typed.

4 Click an article of interest.

■ If additional help articles are available, you can click **more** to view the articles.

■ You may need to use the scroll bar to view the more link.

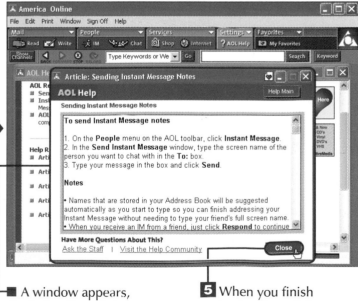

■ A window appears, displaying the article you selected.

5 When you finish reviewing the article, click **Close** to close the window.

BROWSE THROUGH HELP TOPICS

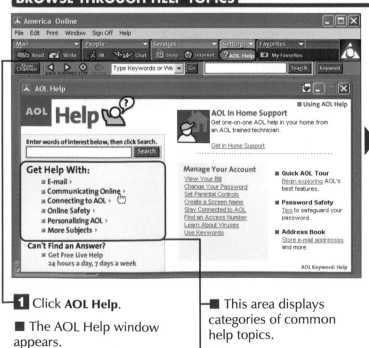

1 Click **AOL Help**.

■ The AOL Help window appears.

■ This area displays categories of common help topics.

2 Click a category of interest.

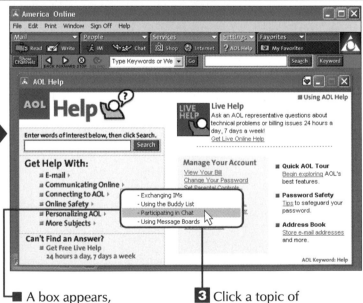

■ A box appears, displaying a list of topics in the category.

3 Click a topic of interest.

■ A window appears.

Can I print a help article?

Yes. You can produce a paper copy of the help article displayed on your screen. This is useful when you want to refer to the article while performing a task.

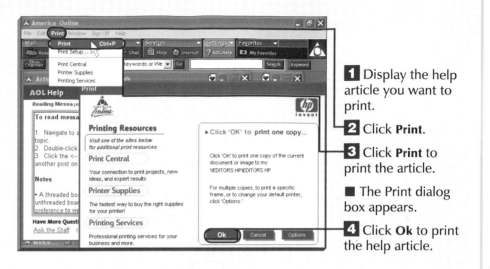

1 Display the help article you want to print.

2 Click **Print**.

3 Click **Print** to print the article.

■ The Print dialog box appears.

4 Click **Ok** to print the help article.

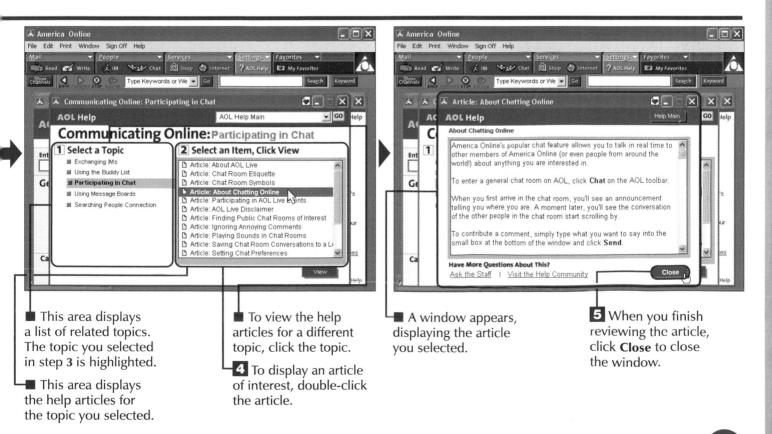

■ This area displays a list of related topics. The topic you selected in step **3** is highlighted.

■ This area displays the help articles for the topic you selected.

■ To view the help articles for a different topic, click the topic.

4 To display an article of interest, double-click the article.

■ A window appears, displaying the article you selected.

5 When you finish reviewing the article, click **Close** to close the window.

CHAPTER 2

FIND INFORMATION ON AOL

Wondering how to navigate through the vast amount of information offered by AOL? In this chapter you will learn how to use channels and keywords to find information of interest.

AOL offers an enormous amount of information that is organized into channels such as Games, News, Sports and Travel. You can display the information for a channel of interest.

AOL constantly changes the information offered on each channel. Make sure you revisit your favorite channels often to view the latest information.

VIEW AOL CHANNELS

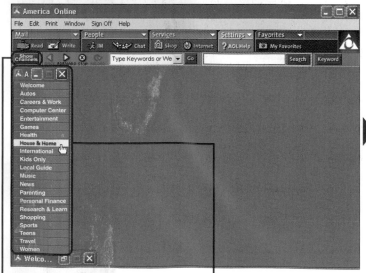

1 To display a list of the channels available on AOL, click **Show Channels**.

Note: The list of channels may already be displayed on your screen. The list automatically appears each time you connect to AOL.

■ The AOL Channels window appears.

2 Click a channel of interest.

■ A window appears, displaying the information for the channel you selected.

■ To view the information for another channel, repeat step **2**.

3 When you finish viewing the information for the channel, click ☒ to close the window.

SELECT A LINK

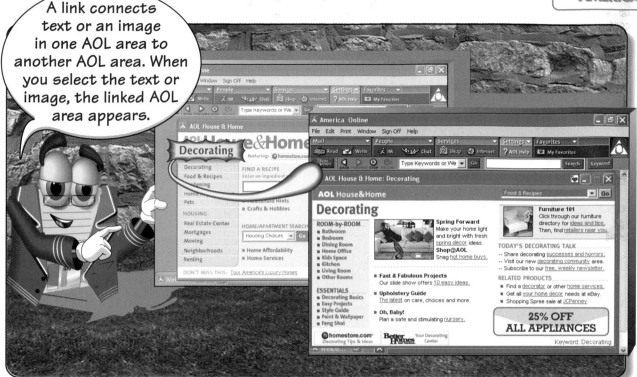

A link connects text or an image in one AOL area to another AOL area. When you select the text or image, the linked AOL area appears.

Links are also known as hyperlinks.

SELECT A LINK

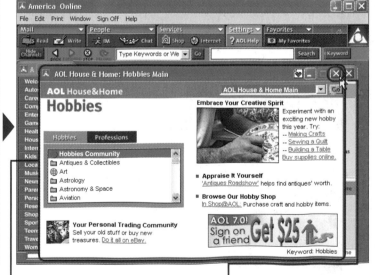

1 Position the mouse ⬉ over a word or image of interest. The mouse ⬉ changes to a hand 🖐 when over a link.

2 Click the word or image to display the linked AOL area.

■ A window appears, displaying the AOL area you selected.

■ You can continue to click links of interest to browse through the information offered by AOL.

3 When you finish viewing the information in a window, click ❌ to close the window.

USING KEYWORDS

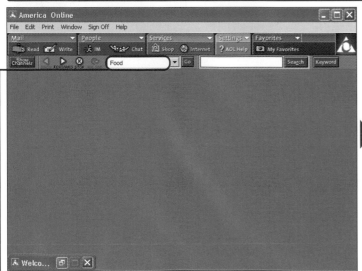

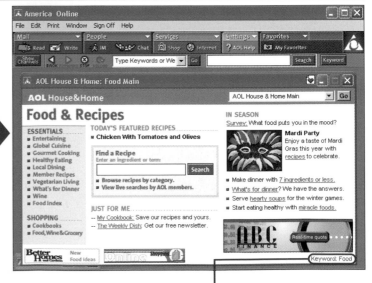

1 Click this area and type the keyword for the AOL area you want to visit. Then press the Enter key.

*Note: If you do not know which keyword to use, try typing a word of interest such as **horoscopes**, **pets** or **stocks**.*

■ The AOL area appears.

■ If an AOL area has a keyword, the keyword will usually be displayed at the bottom of the window.

KEYWORD EXAMPLES

Computing
Computer Center
Computing Community
Download Center
Get Help Now
Online Learning

Entertainment
Books & Arts
Celebrities
Movies
Music
TV

Families
Busy Parents
Family Entertainment
Mom to Mom
Parental Controls
Parents Toolbox

Games
EA Games
Games
Games News
PC Games
Video Games

Health
Alternative Medicine
Children's Health
Conditions
Health Community
Medical Search

Interests
Autos
Food
Hobbies
Home
Pets

News
Business News
News
The Nation
Weather
World News

Personal Finance
Banking
MNC Stocks
My Portfolios
Saving & Planning
Stock

Research & Learn
Fun Facts
History
Homework Help
Online Campus
Research

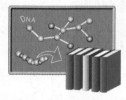

Sports
Golf
Outdoors
Pro Football
Scoreboard
Sports Community

Travel
Destinations
Interests & Activities
Resources & Tips
Travel
Travel Deals

Workplace
Careers & Work
Doing Business Online
Professions
Research a Company
StartUp

You can display a list of all the available keywords on AOL. This is useful when you want to browse through the keywords to find AOL areas of interest.

AOL Keywords: A

A.I.: A.I. Artificial Intelligence

A.I.Movie: A.I. Movie

Aadvantage: AOL AAdvantage Rewards

Aaliyah: Aaliyah

AaronCarter: Aaron Carter

ABabyAtLast: A Baby At Last

AbandonedAuto: Abandoned Cars

ABeautifulMind: A Beautiful Mind

AbrahamLincoln: Abraham Lincoln

Keywords instantly take you to AOL areas.

DISPLAY A LIST OF KEYWORDS

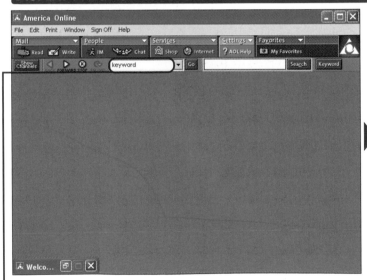

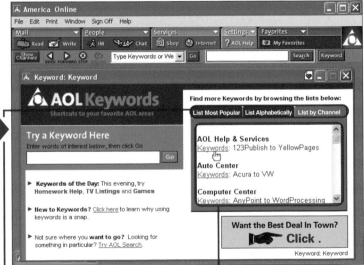

1 Click this area and type **keyword**. Then press the **Enter** key.

■ The Keyword window appears.

2 Click a tab to specify how you want to list the keywords.

Note: For more information, see the top of page 27.

3 Click **Keywords** beside the group of keywords you want to display.

Note: If groups of keywords are not displayed, skip to step 4.

SIMPLIFY IT

How can I display a list of keywords?

eBay
Mapquest
Weather

List Most Popular

Displays the 10 most popular keywords.

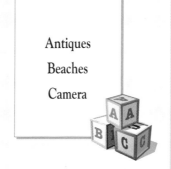

Antiques
Beaches
Camera

List Alphabetically

Displays an alphabetical list of keywords.

Computer Center
Entertainment
Health

List by Channel

Displays a list of keywords organized by channel. AOL organizes information into channels such as Computer Center, Entertainment, Health and News.

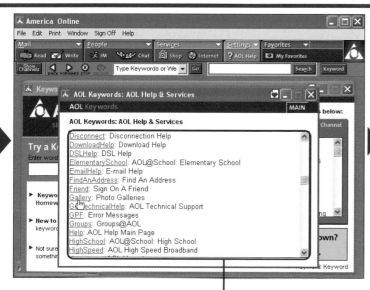

■ A window appears, displaying a list of keywords.

4 Click a keyword of interest.

■ A window appears, displaying the AOL area for the keyword you selected.

■ The window may display the keyword you can use to instantly return to the AOL area at any time.

5 When you finish viewing the AOL area, click ✕ to close the window.

27

CHAPTER 3

BROWSE THE WEB

Do you want to browse through information on the World Wide Web? This chapter will explain how the Web works and how you can use it to transfer information to your computer from Web sites around the world.

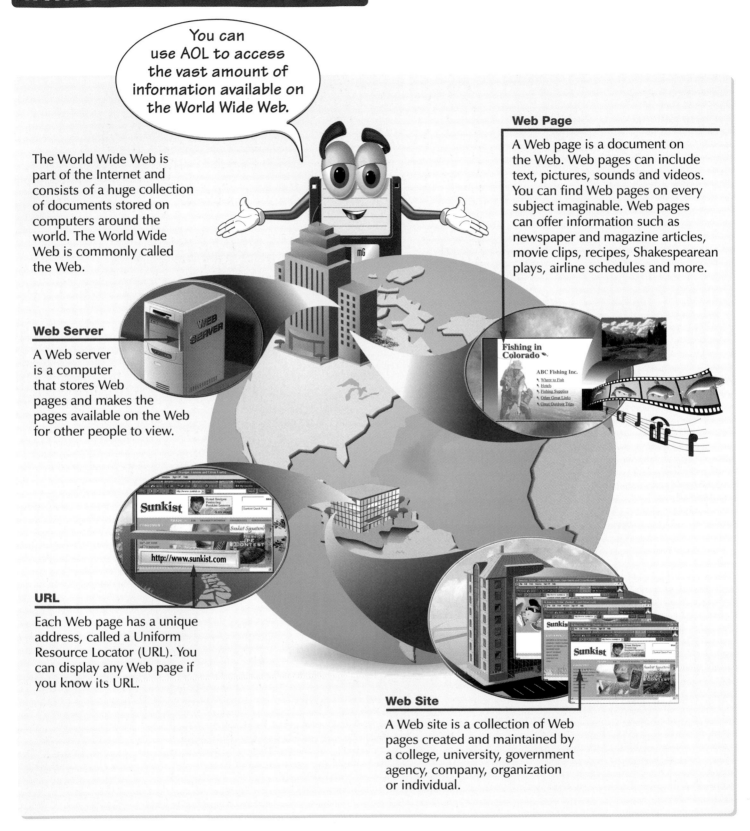

You can use AOL to access the vast amount of information available on the World Wide Web.

The World Wide Web is part of the Internet and consists of a huge collection of documents stored on computers around the world. The World Wide Web is commonly called the Web.

Web Page

A Web page is a document on the Web. Web pages can include text, pictures, sounds and videos. You can find Web pages on every subject imaginable. Web pages can offer information such as newspaper and magazine articles, movie clips, recipes, Shakespearean plays, airline schedules and more.

Web Server

A Web server is a computer that stores Web pages and makes the pages available on the Web for other people to view.

URL

Each Web page has a unique address, called a Uniform Resource Locator (URL). You can display any Web page if you know its URL.

Web Site

A Web site is a collection of Web pages created and maintained by a college, university, government agency, company, organization or individual.

Web Browser

A Web browser is a program that allows you to view and explore information on the Web. AOL includes a built-in Web browser.

Links

Web pages contain links, which are highlighted text or images on a Web page that connect to other pages on the Web. You can select a link to display a Web page located on the same computer or on a computer across the city, country or world. Links are also known as hyperlinks.

Links allow you to easily navigate through a vast amount of information by jumping from one Web page to another. This is known as "browsing the Web."

AOL and the Web

Although you can use AOL to access the Web, you should keep in mind that AOL and the Web are separate. When you browse the Web, you are viewing content outside of AOL. Unlike AOL areas, the content of Web pages is not approved or controlled by AOL.

DISPLAY A SPECIFIC WEB PAGE

You can display a page on the Web that you have heard or read about.

You need to know the address of the Web page you want to view. Each page on the Web has a unique address, called a Uniform Resource Locator (URL).

DISPLAY A SPECIFIC WEB PAGE

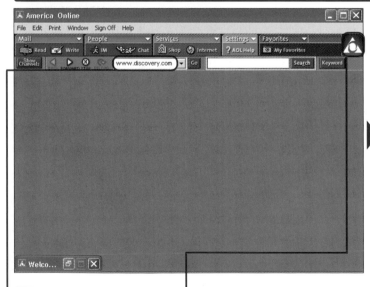

1 Click this area to highlight the current text.

2 Type the address of the Web page you want to display and then press the Enter key.

*Note: You do not need to type **http://** when typing a Web page address.*

■ This icon is animated when information is transferring to your computer.

■ The Web page appears on your screen.

■ This area displays the title of the Web page.

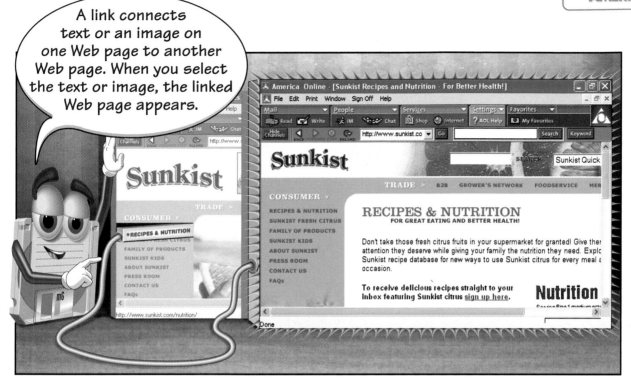

A link connects text or an image on one Web page to another Web page. When you select the text or image, the linked Web page appears.

Links allow you to easily navigate through a vast amount of information by jumping from one Web page to another. Links are also known as hyperlinks.

SELECT A LINK

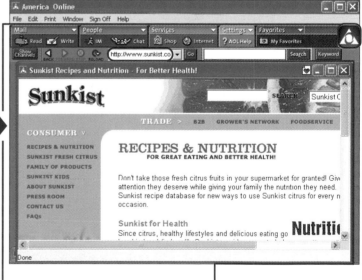

1 Position the mouse over a word or image of interest. The mouse changes to a hand when over a link.

■ This area displays the address of the Web page that the link will take you to.

2 Click the word or image to display the linked Web page.

■ The linked Web page appears.

■ This icon is animated as the Web page transfers to your computer.

■ This area displays the address of the Web page.

You may also want to stop the transfer of a Web page if you realize the page contains information that does not interest you.

STOP TRANSFER OF A WEB PAGE

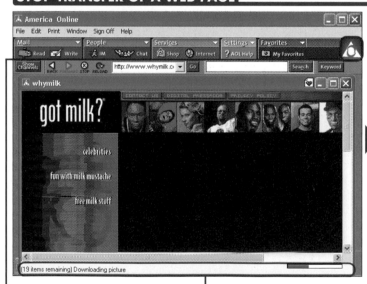

■ This icon is animated as a Web page transfers to your computer.

■ This area shows the progress of the transfer.

1 Click **Stop** to stop the transfer of the Web page.

■ If you stopped the transfer of the Web page because the page was taking too long to appear, you may want to try displaying the page at a later time.

34

RELOAD A WEB PAGE

You can reload a Web page to update the information displayed on the page. A fresh copy of the Web page will transfer to your computer.

Reloading a Web page is useful for updating information such as the current news, sports scores and stock market data.

RELOAD A WEB PAGE

1 Click **Reload** to transfer a fresh copy of the displayed Web page to your computer.

■ A fresh copy of the Web page appears on your screen.

You can easily move back and forth through the Web pages you have viewed since you last started the AOL browser.

You can also move back and forth through AOL areas you have viewed.

MOVE THROUGH WEB PAGES

MOVE BACK

1 Click **Back** to display the last Web page you viewed.

Note: If the Back button is dimmed, you cannot use the button to display a Web page.

MOVE FORWARD

1 Click **Forward** to move forward through the Web pages you have viewed.

Note: The Forward button is only available after you use the Back button to return to a Web page.

RETURN TO A WEB PAGE

RETURN TO A WEB PAGE

1 Click ⬇ in this area to display a list of Web pages you have recently viewed.

2 Click the Web page you want to redisplay.

Note: The list also displays AOL areas you have recently viewed. You can click an AOL area you want to redisplay.

■ The Web page you selected appears on your screen.

SEARCH THE WEB

You can search for Web sites that discuss topics of interest to you.

You can also search AOL areas for information of interest.

SEARCH THE WEB

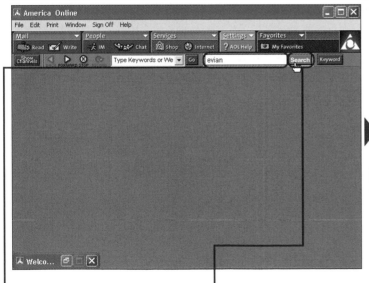

1 Click this area and type a word or phrase that describes the information you want to search for.

2 Click **Search** to start the search.

■ The AOL Search window appears, displaying a list of matching Web sites and their descriptions.

Note: The list may also include matching AOL areas and their descriptions.

Is there another way to search for information on the Web?

Yes. Many Web sites allow you to search for information on the Web. These Web sites can also allow you to browse through categories, such as news, sports and weather, to find Web pages of interest. Here are some popular Web sites that allow you to search for information on the Web.

Google
www.google.com

Lycos
www.lycos.com

Yahoo!
www.yahoo.com

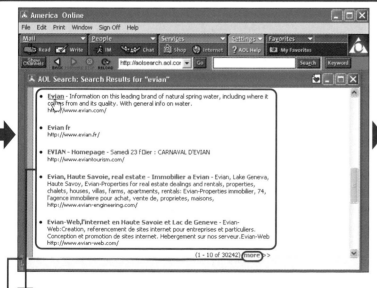

3 To display a Web site, click the Web site of interest.

■ If the list of matching Web sites is more than one page long, you can click **more** to view the next page of matching Web sites.

■ You may need to use the scroll bar to view the **more** link.

■ The Web site you selected appears.

■ You can click **Back** to return to the list of matching Web sites.

CHAPTER 4

READ AND COMPOSE E-MAIL

Would you like to exchange e-mail messages with friends, family members and colleagues from around the world? This chapter will show you how.

To: lucky
Subject: Fishin

Congratulations
I'm looking forward
at the awards ceremony! I've also
included photos from the event in
an attached file.

You can read your e-mail messages to review their contents. You can receive messages from other AOL members and people on the Internet.

AOL deletes messages you have read after about 3 days and messages you have not read after about 27 days. Messages are automatically deleted to keep the AOL computer system from overflowing with messages.

READ MESSAGES

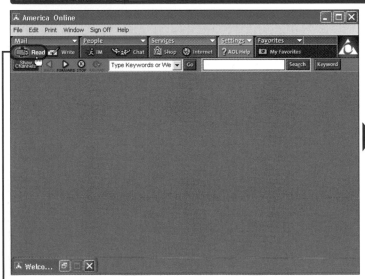

■ When you have new messages, the flag on this mailbox is up.

1 Click **Read** to read your messages.

■ The Online Mailbox window appears.

2 Click the tab for the messages you want to read.

New Mail
Displays new messages.

Old Mail
Displays messages you have previously read.

Sent Mail
Displays messages you have sent.

What is my e-mail address?

Your e-mail address defines the location of your mailbox. The e-mail address a person will use to send you a message depends on whether the person is an AOL member or an Internet user.

AOL Members

When another AOL member sends you a message, the member addresses the message using your screen name, such as johnsmith.

Internet Users

When a person on the Internet sends you a message, the person addresses the message using your screen name followed by @aol.com, such as johnsmith@aol.com.

How can I tell if a person who sent me an e-mail message is online?

If the person is an AOL member, this icon 🚶 will appear beside the person's screen name at the top of the message when they are online.

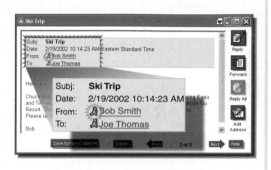

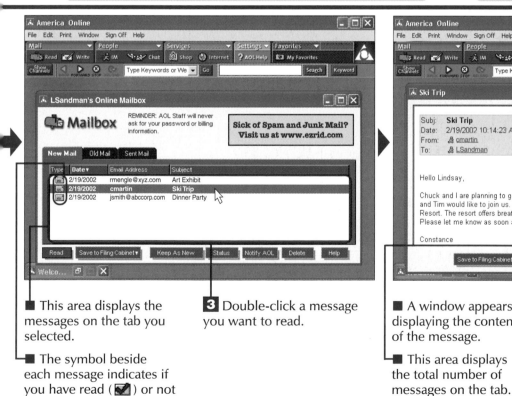

■ This area displays the messages on the tab you selected.

■ The symbol beside each message indicates if you have read (✔) or not read (📩) the message.

3 Double-click a message you want to read.

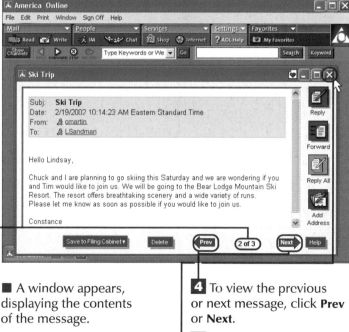

■ A window appears, displaying the contents of the message.

■ This area displays the total number of messages on the tab.

4 To view the previous or next message, click **Prev** or **Next**.

5 When you finish reading your messages, click ✖ to close the window.

To practice sending a message, you can send a message to yourself.

SEND A MESSAGE

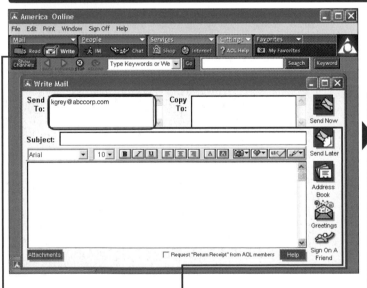

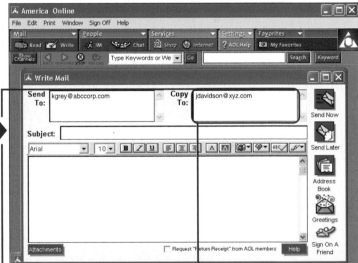

1 Click **Write** to send a new message.

■ The Write Mail window appears.

2 Type the e-mail address or screen name of the person you want to receive the message.

*Note: To select an e-mail address or screen name from the address book, see page 58. Then skip to step **4**.*

3 To send a copy of the message to another person, click this area and then type the person's e-mail address or screen name.

■ To send a blind copy, enclose the e-mail address or screen name in brackets ( ).

*Note: To send the message to more than one person in step **2** or **3**, separate each e-mail address or screen name with a comma (,).*

How can I address a message I want to send?

Send To

Send the message to the person you specify.

Copy To

Send an exact copy of the message to a person who is not directly involved but would be interested in the message.

Blind Copy

Send an exact copy of the message to a person without anyone else knowing that the person received the message.

How can I express emotions in my e-mail messages?

You can use special characters, called smileys, to express emotions in e-mail messages. These characters resemble human faces if you turn them sideways.

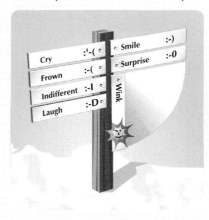

Cry	:'-(	Smile :-)
Frown	:-(	Surprise :-0
Indifferent	:-l	Wink
Laugh	:-D	

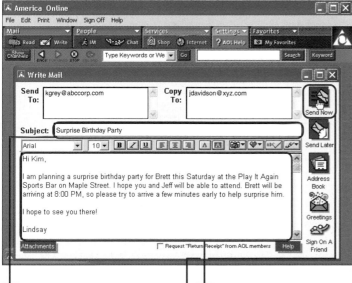

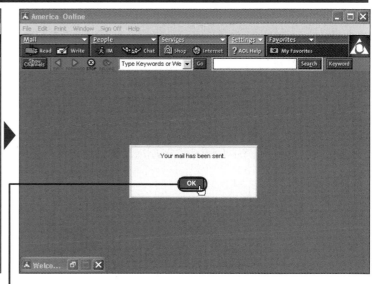

4 Click this area and then type the subject of the message.

Note: The subject should clearly describe the contents of the message.

5 Click this area and then type the message.

6 Click **Send Now** to send the message.

■ A dialog box appears, confirming the message was sent.

7 Click **OK** to close the dialog box.

■ The AOL software stores a copy of the message on the Sent Mail tab. For information about the mail tabs, see page 42.

You can include all or part of the original message in your reply to help the reader identify which message you are replying to. This is called quoting.

REPLY TO A MESSAGE

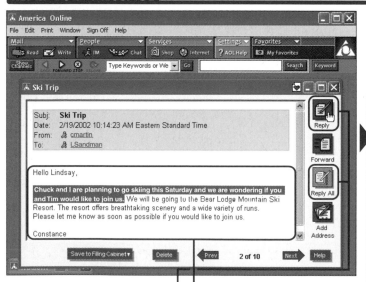

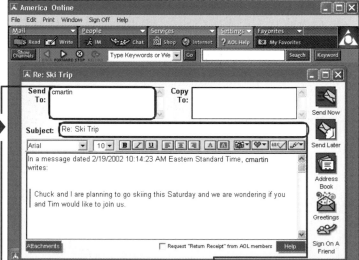

1 Display the contents of the message you want to reply to. To display the contents of a message, see page 42.

2 To include all or part of the original message in your reply, drag the mouse I over the text you want to include until you highlight the text.

3 Click the reply option you want to use.

Note: For information about the reply options, see the top of page 47.

■ A window appears for you to compose your reply.

■ The AOL software fills in the e-mail address(es) or screen name(s) for you.

■ The AOL software also fills in the subject, starting the subject with **Re:**.

How can I reply to a message?

Reply

Send a reply to only the author.

Reply All

Send a reply to the author and everyone who received the original message.

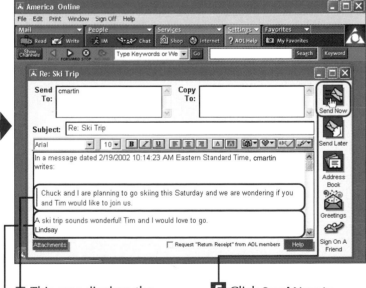

 What should I consider when composing my reply?

A MESSAGE WRITTEN IN CAPITAL LETTERS IS ANNOYING AND DIFFICULT TO READ. THIS IS CALLED SHOUTING. Always use upper and lower case letters when typing e-mail messages.

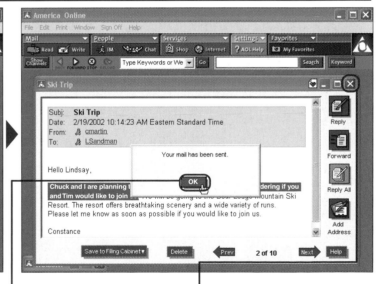

■ This area displays the text you included from the original message.

4 Click this area and then type your reply.

5 Click **Send Now** to send your reply.

■ A dialog box appears, confirming the message was sent.

6 Click **OK** to close the dialog box.

7 Click ✕ to close the window that displays the contents of the original message.

■ The AOL software stores a copy of the message on the Sent Mail tab. For information about the mail tabs, see page 42.

After reading a message, you can add comments and then forward the message to a friend, family member or colleague.

Forwarding a message is useful when you know another person would be interested in the message.

FORWARD A MESSAGE

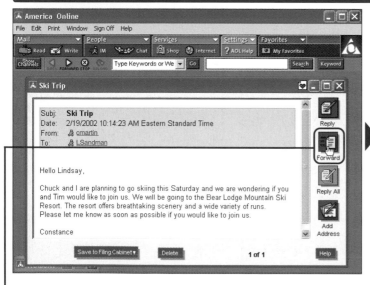

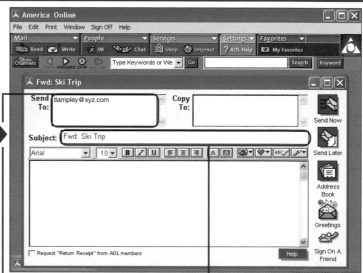

1 Display the contents of the message you want to forward. To display the contents of a message, see page 42.

2 Click **Forward** to forward the message.

■ A window appears for you to enter your comments.

Note: Although the window does not display the contents of the message you are forwarding, the recipient will be able to see the contents of the message.

3 Type the e-mail address or screen name of the person you want to receive the message.

Note: To select an e-mail address or screen name from the address book, see page 58.

■ The AOL software fills in the subject for you, starting the subject with **Fwd:**.

How do I forward a message to more than one person?

When forwarding a message, you can type the e-mail address or screen name of each person you want to receive the message. Make sure you separate each e-mail address or screen name with a comma (,).

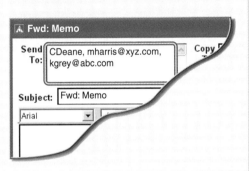

How can I save time when typing a message?

You can use abbreviations for words and phrases to save time when typing messages. Here are some commonly used abbreviations.

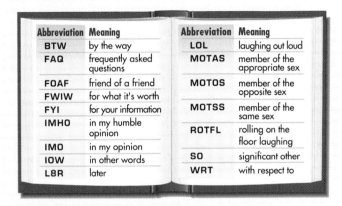

Abbreviation	Meaning	Abbreviation	Meaning
BTW	by the way	LOL	laughing out loud
FAQ	frequently asked questions	MOTAS	member of the appropriate sex
FOAF	friend of a friend	MOTOS	member of the opposite sex
FWIW	for what it's worth		
FYI	for your information	MOTSS	member of the same sex
IMHO	in my humble opinion	ROTFL	rolling on the floor laughing
IMO	in my opinion		
IOW	in other words	SO	significant other
L8R	later	WRT	with respect to

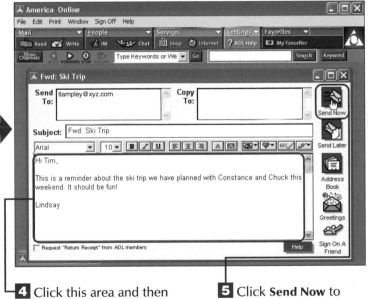

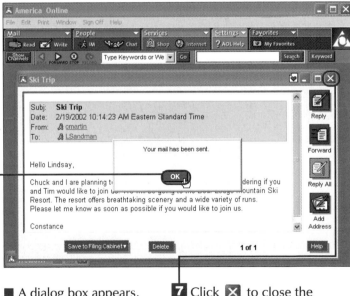

4 Click this area and then type any comments about the message you are forwarding.

5 Click **Send Now** to forward the message.

■ A dialog box appears, confirming the message was sent.

6 Click **OK** to close the dialog box.

7 Click ☒ to close the window that displays the contents of the original message.

■ The AOL software stores a copy of the message on the Sent Mail tab. For information about the mail tabs, see page 42.

BOLD, ITALICIZE OR UNDERLINE TEXT

BOLD, ITALICIZE OR UNDERLINE TEXT

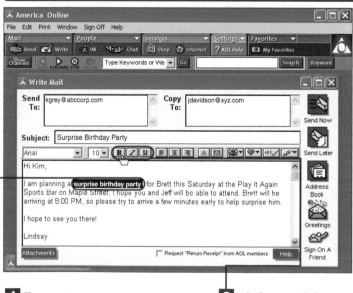

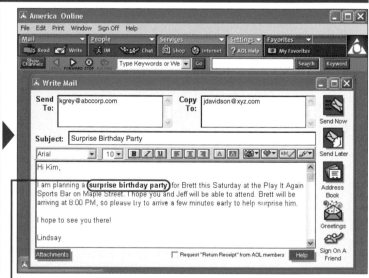

1 To create a message, perform steps **1** to **5** starting on page 44.

2 To select the text you want to bold, italicize or underline, drag the mouse I over the text until the text is highlighted.

3 Click one of the following buttons.

B Bold

I Italics

U Underline

■ The text you selected appears in the new style.

■ To deselect text, click outside the selected area.

■ To remove a bold, italic or underline style, repeat steps **2** and **3**.

You can change the color of text in a message to help draw attention to important information.

CHANGE COLOR OF TEXT

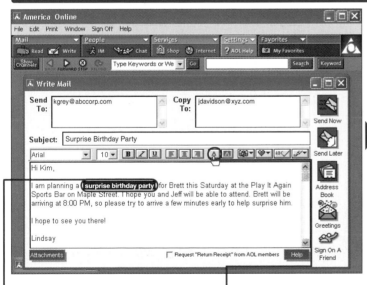

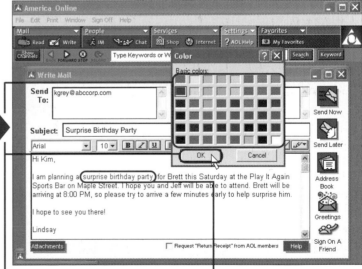

1 To create a message, perform steps **1** to **5** starting on page 44.

2 To select the text you want to change to a different color, drag the mouse ⌶ over the text until the text is highlighted.

3 Click 🅰 to display the available colors.

■ The Color dialog box appears.

4 Click the color you want to use.

5 Click **OK** to confirm your selection.

■ The text you selected appears in the new color.

■ To deselect text, click outside the selected area.

SPELL CHECK A MESSAGE

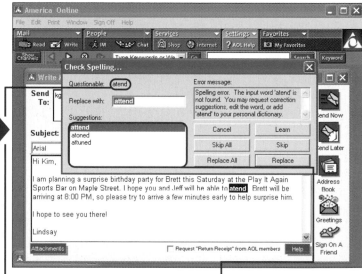

1 To create a message, perform steps **1** to **5** starting on page 44.

2 To start the spell check at the beginning of your message, click to the left of the first character in the message.

3 Click **Edit**.

4 Click **Spell Check** to start the spell check.

■ The Check Spelling dialog box appears if your message contains a spelling error.

■ This area displays the first misspelled word.

■ This area displays suggestions for correcting the word.

Will the AOL software find all the spelling errors in my message?

The AOL software compares every word in your message to words in its dictionary. If a word does not exist in the dictionary, the word is considered misspelled. The AOL software will not find a correctly spelled word used in the wrong context, such as "The girl is **sit** years old." You should carefully review your message to find this type of error.

Can I spell check other types of messages?

In addition to e-mail messages, you can spell check instant messages and messages you want to send to a message board. Compose the message you want to send and then perform steps **2** to **8** below to spell check the message. For information about sending an instant message, see page 84. For information about sending a message to a message board, see page 126.

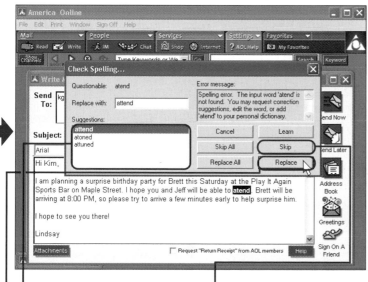

5 Click the suggestion you want to use to correct the misspelled word.

6 Click **Replace** to correct the misspelled word.

■ To skip the word and continue checking your message, click **Skip**.

*Note: To skip the word and all other occurrences of the word in your message, click **Skip All**.*

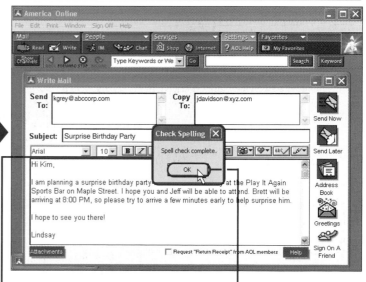

7 Replace or skip misspelled words until this dialog box appears, telling you the spell check is complete.

8 Click **OK** to close the dialog box.

ADD A NAME TO THE ADDRESS BOOK

> You can use the address book to store the e-mail addresses and screen names of people you frequently send messages to.

Selecting a name from the address book helps you avoid typing mistakes when entering an e-mail address or screen name. Typing mistakes can result in a message being delivered to the wrong person or being returned to you.

ADD A NAME TO THE ADDRESS BOOK

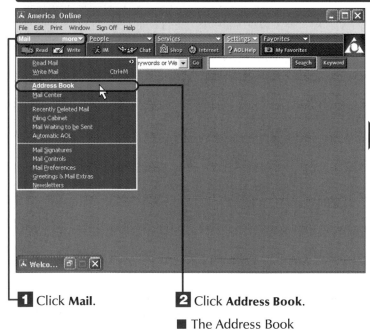

1 Click **Mail**.

2 Click **Address Book**.

■ The Address Book window appears.

3 Click **Add Contact** to add a name to the address book.

■ The Contact Details window appears.

4 Type the first name of the person you want to add to the address book.

5 Click this area and then type the last name of the person.

Is there another way to add a name to the address book?

Yes. When reading an e-mail message, you can click the **Add Address** button ( ) to quickly add the sender of the message to the address book. AOL displays the Contact Details window and automatically fills in the sender's e-mail address for you. If the sender is an AOL member, AOL will also add the person's screen name. You can enter additional information for the person and then click the **Save** button to add the person to the address book.

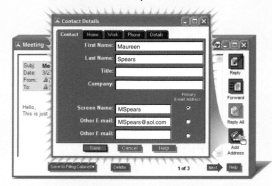

How do I delete a name from the address book?

To delete a name from the address book, click the name in the Address Book window and then press the Delete key. In the confirmation dialog box that appears, click **Yes** to confirm the deletion.

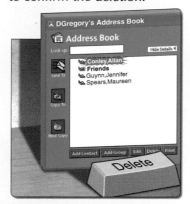

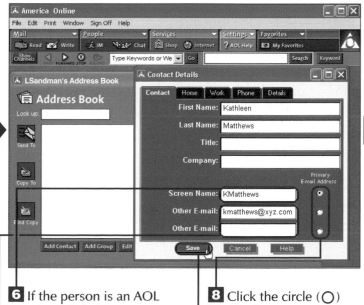

6 If the person is an AOL member, click this area and type the person's screen name.

7 If the person has other e-mail addresses, you can click each area and type an e-mail address.

8 Click the circle (○) beside the screen name or e-mail address you want AOL to use when you select the person's name from the address book (○ changes to ⊙).

9 Click **Save** to add the person's name to the address book.

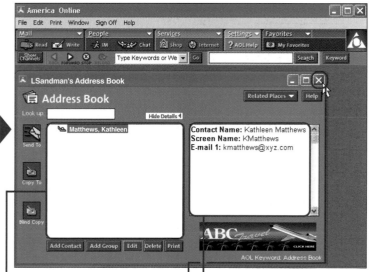

■ The person's name appears in this area of the Address Book window.

■ The person's information appears in this area of the Address Book window.

10 Click ✕ to close the Address Book window.

ADD A GROUP TO THE ADDRESS BOOK

You can add a group to your address book so you can quickly send the same message to every person in the group.

You can create as many groups as you need. A person can belong to more than one group.

ADD A GROUP TO THE ADDRESS BOOK

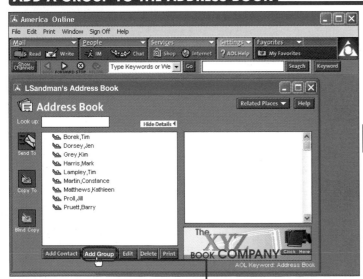

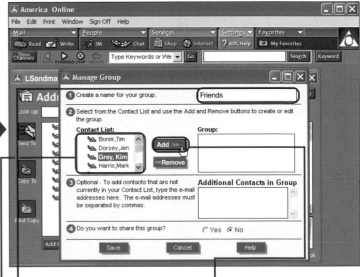

1 Perform steps **1** and **2** on page 54 to display the Address Book window.

2 Click **Add Group** to add a new group to the address book.

■ The Manage Group window appears.

3 Type a name for the group.

■ This area displays the names of the people in your address book.

4 Click the name of a person you want to include in the group.

5 Click **Add** to include the person in the group.

6 Repeat steps **4** and **5** for each person you want to include in the group.

Can I make changes to a group I added to the address book?

Yes. In the Address Book window, click the name of the group you want to change and then click the **Edit** button to display the Manage Group window. You can then perform steps **4** to **10** below to add or remove people in the group.

How do I delete a group from the address book?

To delete a group from the address book, click the name of the group in the Address Book window and then click the **Delete** button. In the confirmation dialog box that appears, click **Yes** to delete the group. The AOL software will not remove the people in the group from your address book.

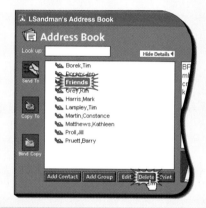

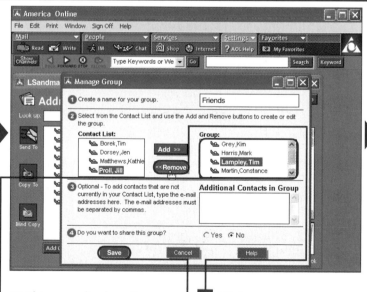

■ This area displays the name of each person you included in the group.

7 To remove a person you accidentally included in the group, click the name of the person in this area.

8 Click **Remove** to remove the person from the group.

9 When you finish selecting all the people you want to include in the group, click **Save**.

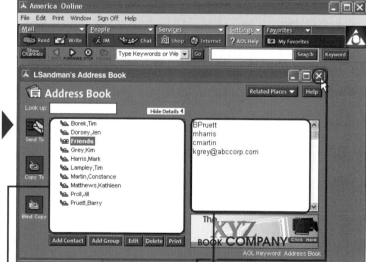

■ The name of the group appears in this area of the Address Book window.

■ A group displays the 👥 symbol. An individual name displays the 👤 symbol.

■ The e-mail address or screen name of each person in the group appears in this area of the Address Book window.

10 Click **X** to close the Address Book window.

When sending a message, you can select the name of the person you want to receive the message from the address book.

Selecting names from the address book saves you from having to remember the e-mail addresses and screen names of people you often send messages to.

You can select a group from the address book the same way you select a name from the address book. When you select a group, AOL sends the message to every person in the group.

SELECT A NAME FROM THE ADDRESS BOOK

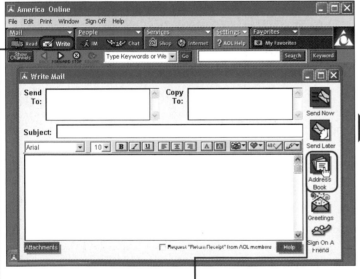

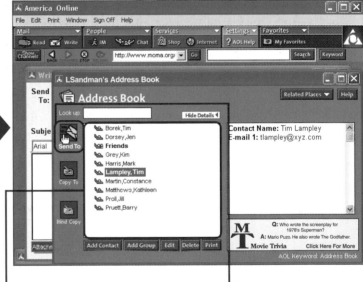

1 Click **Write** to send a new message.

■ The Write Mail window appears.

2 Click **Address Book** to select a name from the address book.

■ The Address Book window appears.

3 Click the name of the person you want to receive the message.

4 Click **Send To**.

■ You can repeat steps **3** and **4** for each person you want to receive the message.

Is there a faster way to select a name from the address book?

Yes. When you are addressing a message, AOL may display a list of suggestions to help you quickly select a name from the address book.

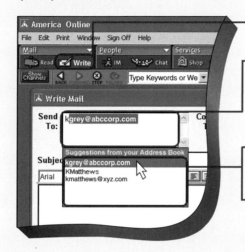

1 Click **Write** to display the Write Mail window.

2 Click the **Send To** area and then type the first few letters of the person's name, e-mail address or screen name.

■ A list of e-mail addresses and screen names from the address book appears.

3 Click the e-mail address or screen name you want to use.

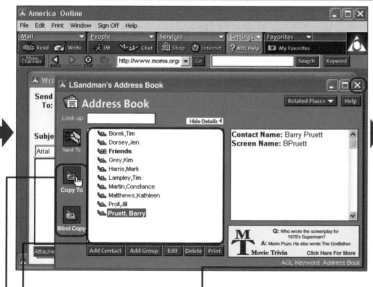

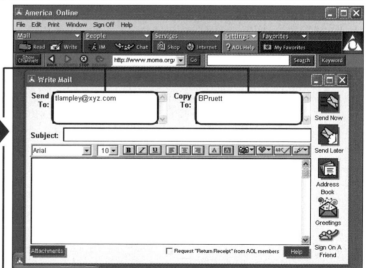

5 To send a copy or blind copy of the message to another person, click the name of the person.

6 Click **Copy To** or **Blind Copy**.

Note: For information about sending a copy or blind copy, see the top of page 45.

■ You can repeat steps **5** and **6** for each person you want to receive a copy or blind copy of the message.

7 Click ✕ to close the Address Book window.

■ These areas display the e-mail address or screen name of each person you selected from the address book.

Note: Brackets ( ) appear around the e-mail address or screen name of each person who will receive a blind copy.

■ To complete the message, perform steps **4** to **7** on page 45.

You can attach a file to a message you are sending. Attaching a file to a message is useful when you want to include additional information with the message.

ATTACH A FILE TO A MESSAGE

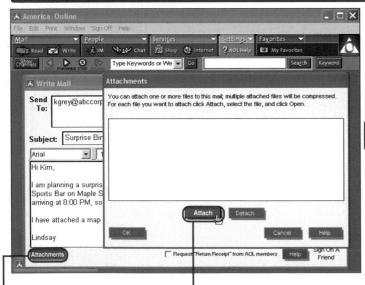

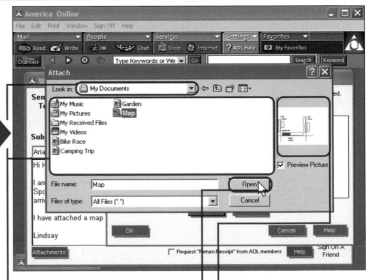

1 To create a message, perform steps **1** to **5** starting on page 44.

2 Click **Attachments** to attach a file to the message.

■ The Attachments dialog box appears.

3 Click **Attach** to select the file you want to attach.

■ The Attach dialog box appears.

■ This area shows the location of the displayed files. You can click this area to change the location.

4 Click the name of the file you want to attach to the message.

■ If you selected an image in step **4**, this area displays a preview of the image.

5 Click **Open** to attach the file to the message.

What types of files can I attach to a message?

You can attach many types of files to a message, including documents, images, videos, sounds and programs. The computer receiving the message must have the necessary hardware and software installed to display or play the file you attach.

Does AOL limit the size of files I can attach to a message?

Yes. AOL limits the total size of files you can attach to a message to 16 MB. Keep in mind, however, that when you send a message to a person on the Internet, the person's Internet service provider may not allow them to receive large attachments.

■ The file you selected appears in this area.

■ To attach additional files to the message, perform steps **3** to **5** for each file you want to attach.

Note: If you attach more than one file to the message, the AOL software will compress the files. For information about compressed files, see the top of page 63.

6 Click **OK**.

■ This area displays the name of the attached file.

7 Click **Send Now** to send the message.

■ The File Transfer window will appear, showing the progress of the transfer.

*Note: A dialog box will appear when the file transfer is complete. Click **OK** to close the dialog box.*

Attached files can contain text, images, videos, sounds or programs. Your computer must have the necessary hardware and software installed to display or play the files you receive.

You should download only files you receive from people you trust.

DOWNLOAD AN ATTACHED FILE

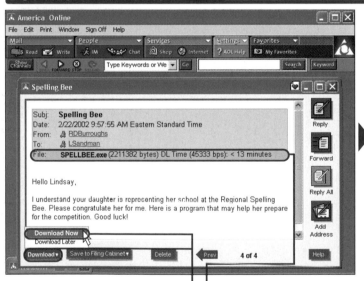

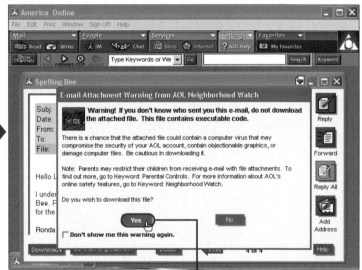

1 Display the contents of a message with an attached file. To display the contents of a message, see page 42.

Note: A message with an attached file displays the 🖳 *symbol.*

■ This area displays information about the attached file.

2 Click **Download**. A menu appears.

3 Click **Download Now** to transfer the file to your computer.

■ A warning appears, stating that you should be cautious about downloading the file if you do not know who sent you the message.

Note: The file may contain offensive pictures or a virus that could damage the information on your computer.

4 Click **Yes** to download the file.

Do I need to check the files I download for viruses?

You should use an anti-virus program to check the files you download for viruses, even if the files are from people you trust. A virus is a program that can damage the information stored on your computer. You can use the keyword **virus** to learn more about viruses and get the latest anti-virus software. For information about using keywords, see page 24.

How do I download a compressed file?

When an AOL member sends you a message with more than one attached file, the AOL software compresses, or squeezes, the files to save storage space and speed up the transfer of information. A compressed file ends with the .zip extension, such as report.zip. You can download a compressed file the same way you download any attached file. When you download a compressed file, the AOL software automatically decompresses the file for you.

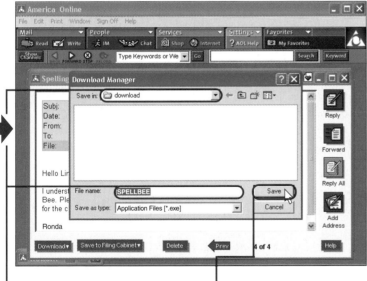

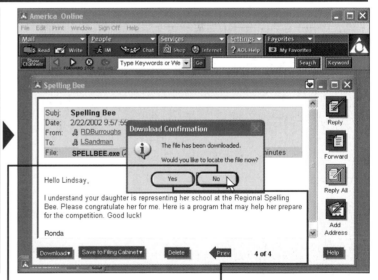

■ The Download Manager dialog box appears.

5 This area displays the name of the file. To use a different name, type a new name.

■ This area shows the location where the file will be stored. You can click this area to change the location.

6 Click **Save** to download the file.

■ The File Transfer window will appear, showing the progress of the transfer.

■ When the transfer is complete, a dialog box may appear, asking if you want to locate the file on your computer.

7 Click **No** to locate the file later. To locate files you have downloaded, see page 204.

■ To locate the file now, click **Yes**. A window will appear, displaying the contents of the folder that contains the file.

Note: The contents of some files will automatically appear on your screen.

CHAPTER 5

WORK WITH E-MAIL

Do you want to learn more about working with e-mail messages? In this chapter you will learn how to save messages, recover messages you accidentally deleted and unsend messages you have second thoughts about sending.

You can save a message that contains information you want to keep.

AOL will keep messages you have read for about 3 days and messages you have not read for about 27 days. If you want to permanently keep a message, you must save the message.

SAVE A MESSAGE

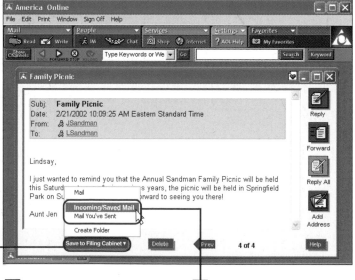

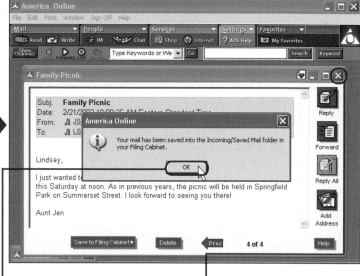

1 Display the contents of the message you want to save. To display the contents of a message, see page 42.

2 Click **Save to Filing Cabinet**. A menu appears.

Note: This button may be named ***Save*** *in some messages.*

3 Click an option to specify the folder you want to store the message.

Incoming/Saved Mail
Stores messages you have received.

Mail You've Sent
Stores messages you have sent.

■ A confirmation dialog box appears, stating that the message was saved.

4 Click **OK** to close the dialog box.

5 Click **X** to close the window that displays the contents of the message.

■ To use the filing cabinet to view saved messages, see page 206.

PRINT A MESSAGE

You can produce a paper copy of the message displayed on your screen.

A printed message includes the page number and total number of pages at the top of each page. The date and your screen name are displayed at the bottom of each page.

PRINT A MESSAGE

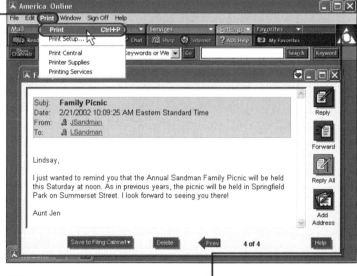

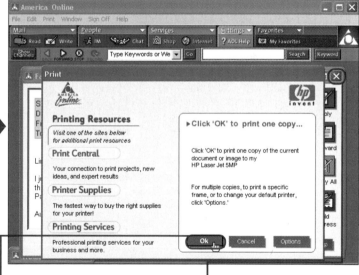

1 Display the contents of the message you want to print. To display the contents of a message, see page 42.

2 Click **Print**.

3 Click **Print** to print the message.

■ The Print dialog box appears.

4 Click **Ok** to print the message.

5 Click **X** to close the window that displays the contents of the message.

AOL automatically deletes messages you have read after about 3 days. Messages you have not read are deleted after about 27 days. If you want to keep messages for a longer period of time, see page 66 to save the messages.

DELETE A MESSAGE

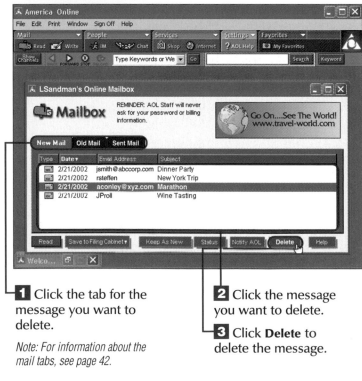

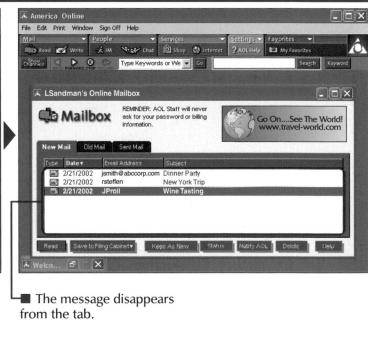

1 Click the tab for the message you want to delete.

Note: For information about the mail tabs, see page 42.

2 Click the message you want to delete.

3 Click **Delete** to delete the message.

■ The message disappears from the tab.

You can recover a message you accidentally deleted from your mailbox.

You can only recover messages you have deleted in the last 24 hours.

RECOVER A DELETED MESSAGE

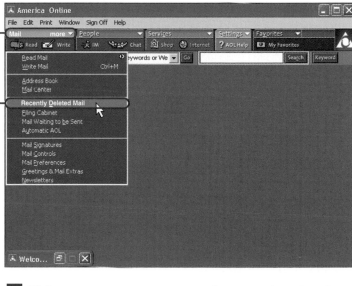

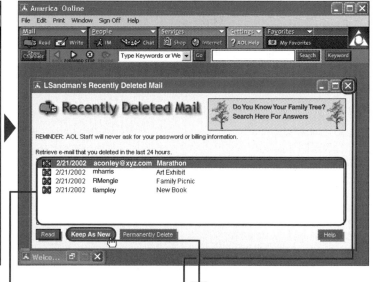

1 Click **Mail**.

2 Click **Recently Deleted Mail**.

■ The Recently Deleted Mail window appears.

■ This area lists the messages you have deleted in the last 24 hours.

3 Click the message you want to recover.

4 Click **Keep As New**.

■ The message will appear as a new message in your mailbox. For information about reading messages, see page 42.

5 Click ☒ to close the Recently Deleted Mail window.

AOL will keep messages you have read for about 3 days and messages you have not read for about 27 days.

MARK A MESSAGE AS NEW

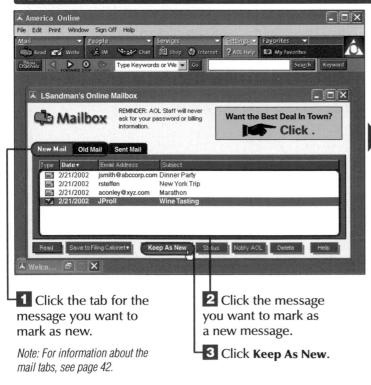

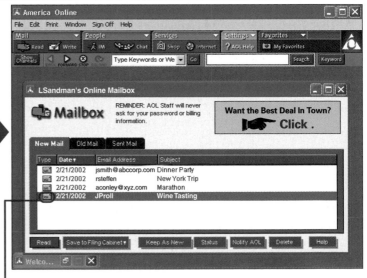

1 Click the tab for the message you want to mark as new.

Note: For information about the mail tabs, see page 42.

2 Click the message you want to mark as a new message.

3 Click **Keep As New**.

■ The symbol beside the message changes from to to indicate the message is new.

■ When you mark a message on the Old Mail tab as new, AOL will move the message to the New Mail tab the next time you read your messages.

CHANGE HOW LONG AOL KEEPS READ MESSAGES

You can specify the number of days AOL will keep messages you have read.

AOL initially stores messages you have read for about 3 days. You can have AOL store read messages for a maximum of 7 days. Unread messages are stored for about 27 days.

CHANGE HOW LONG AOL KEEPS READ MESSAGES

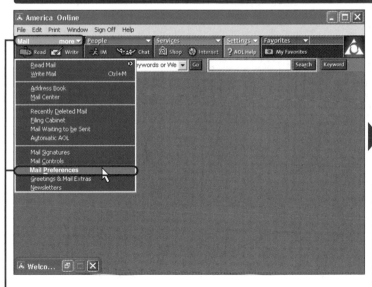

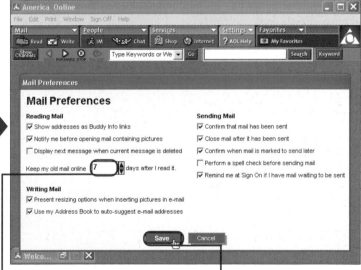

1 Click **Mail**.

2 Click **Mail Preferences**.

■ The Mail Preferences dialog box appears.

■ This area displays how long AOL will keep messages you have read.

3 To change the number of days AOL will keep read messages, double-click this area and type a number from **1** to **7** to specify a new number of days.

4 Click **Save** to save your change.

You can check the status of a message you sent to another AOL member to determine if the member has read the message.

Message has been read.

You cannot check the status of a message you have sent to an Internet address.

CHECK THE STATUS OF A MESSAGE

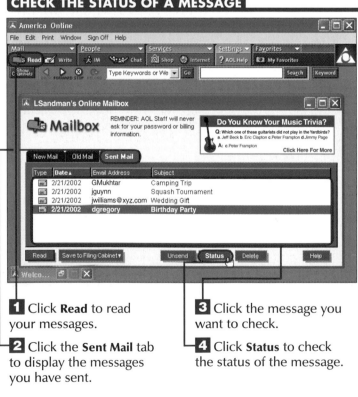

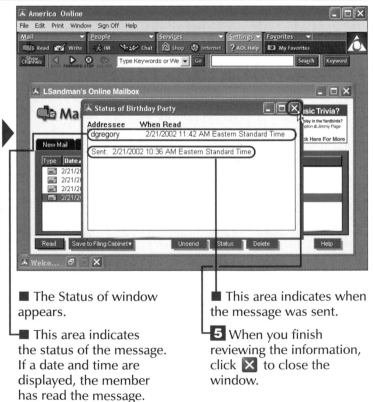

1 Click **Read** to read your messages.

2 Click the **Sent Mail** tab to display the messages you have sent.

3 Click the message you want to check.

4 Click **Status** to check the status of the message.

■ The Status of window appears.

■ This area indicates the status of the message. If a date and time are displayed, the member has read the message.

Note: If the text (not yet read) appears, the member has not yet read the message.

■ This area indicates when the message was sent.

5 When you finish reviewing the information, click ⊠ to close the window.

UNSEND A MESSAGE

You can unsend a message you sent to another AOL member. Unsending a message is useful when you have sent a message to the wrong person or you have second thoughts about the message.

If a message you sent to an AOL member has already been read, you cannot unsend the message.

You cannot unsend a message you have sent to an Internet address.

UNSEND A MESSAGE

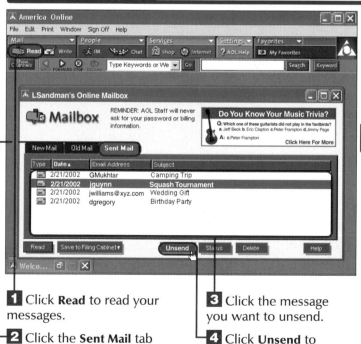

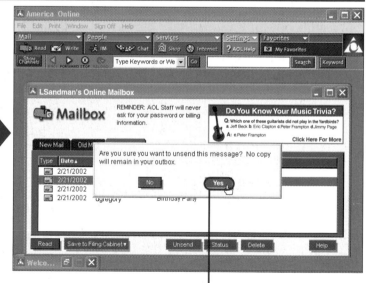

1 Click **Read** to read your messages.

2 Click the **Sent Mail** tab to display the messages you have sent.

3 Click the message you want to unsend.

4 Click **Unsend** to unsend the message.

■ A confirmation dialog box appears.

Note: A different dialog box appears if you try to unsend a message that has already been read. Click OK to close the dialog box.

5 Click **Yes** to unsend the message.

■ A confirmation dialog box will appear. Click **OK** to close the dialog box.

If you do not want to immediately send a message you create, you can send the message later. This is useful when you want to review the message again before sending the message.

Sending a message later allows you to create a message when you are not connected to AOL and then send the message when you later connect. This is useful if you want to keep your telephone line free while you create messages.

Send Later

SEND A MESSAGE LATER

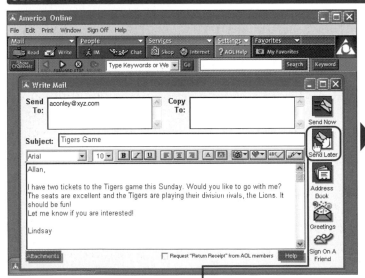

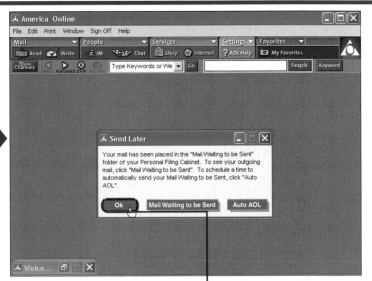

STORE A MESSAGE FOR LATER

1 To create a message, perform steps **1** to **5** starting on page 44.

2 Click **Send Later** to send the message at a later time.

■ The Send Later window appears, stating that your message was placed in the Mail Waiting to be Sent folder.

Note: The Mail Waiting to be Sent folder is located in the filing cabinet. For information about the filing cabinet, see page 206.

3 Click **OK** to close the window.

SIMPLIFY IT

Will AOL notify me when I have messages waiting to be sent?

When you have messages waiting to be sent, a dialog box will appear when you connect to AOL. You can click one of the following options.

Mail Waiting To Be Sent

You have mail waiting to be sent.

To send all of the mail, click Send Now. To review the mail waiting, click Review Mail. To send the mail later, click Send Later.

☐ **Do not ask me again**

[Send Now] [Review Mail] [Send Later]

Send Later

Send all the messages later.

Send Now

Send all the messages now.

Review Mail

View the messages waiting to be sent.

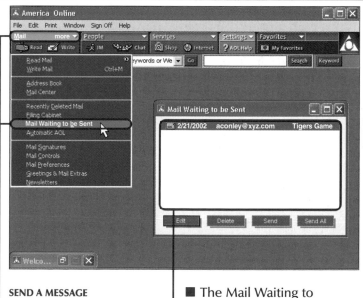

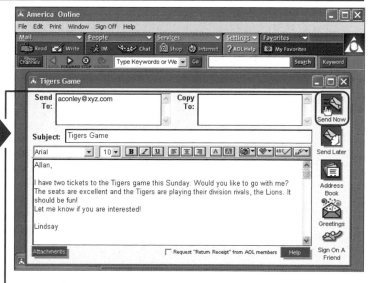

SEND A MESSAGE

1 Click **Mail**.

2 Click **Mail Waiting to be Sent**.

■ The Mail Waiting to be Sent window appears.

3 Double-click the message you want to send.

■ A window appears, displaying the contents of the message. You can review and make changes to the message.

4 To send the message, click **Send Now**.

■ A dialog box will appear, confirming that the message was sent. Click **OK** to close the dialog box.

ADD A SIGNATURE TO MESSAGES

> You can automatically add personal information to the end of every message you send. This information is called a signature.

A signature saves you from having to type the same information every time you send a message.

ADD A SIGNATURE TO MESSAGES

1 Click **Mail**.

2 Click **Mail Signatures**.

■ The Set up Signatures window appears.

3 Click **Create** to create a signature.

What information can I include in a signature?

A signature can include information such as your name, e-mail address, occupation, favorite quotation or Web page address. You can also use plain characters to display simple pictures in your signature. As a courtesy to people who will receive your messages, you should limit your signature to four or five lines.

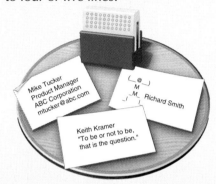

How do I delete a signature?

You can delete a signature you no longer want to appear in every message you send.

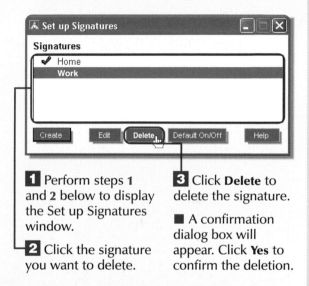

1 Perform steps **1** and **2** below to display the Set up Signatures window.

2 Click the signature you want to delete.

3 Click **Delete** to delete the signature.

■ A confirmation dialog box will appear. Click **Yes** to confirm the deletion.

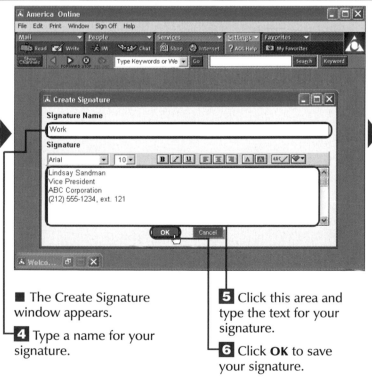

■ The Create Signature window appears.

4 Type a name for your signature.

5 Click this area and type the text for your signature.

6 Click **OK** to save your signature.

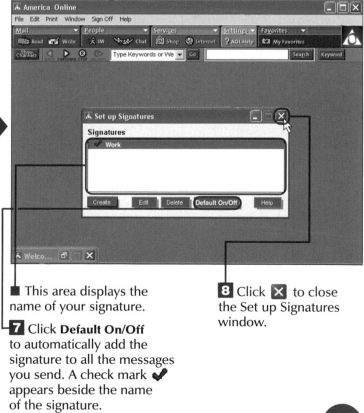

■ This area displays the name of your signature.

7 Click **Default On/Off** to automatically add the signature to all the messages you send. A check mark ✔ appears beside the name of the signature.

8 Click ✕ to close the Set up Signatures window.

CHAPTER 6

USING THE BUDDY LIST

Would you like to know when your friends, family members and colleagues are online? In this chapter you will learn how to use the Buddy List to determine when a person is online so you can send them an instant message.

You can add a friend, family member or colleague to the Buddy List. The Buddy List allows you to quickly determine when a person is online so you can communicate with them.

AOL provides three groups in the Buddy List—Buddies, Family and Co-Workers. You can add AOL members to these groups at any time.

ADD A BUDDY

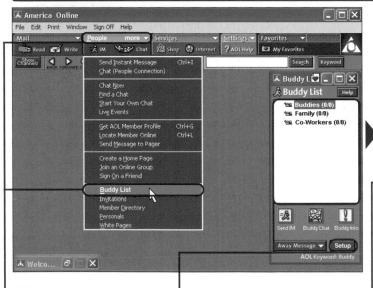

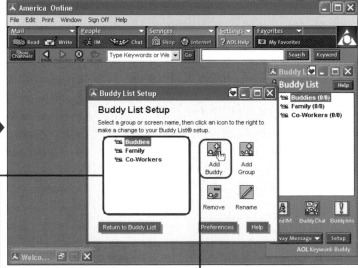

1 Click **People**.

2 Click **Buddy List**.

■ The Buddy List window appears.

Note: The Buddy List window may already be displayed on your screen. The window automatically appears each time you connect to AOL.

■ This area displays the name of each group in the Buddy List.

3 Click **Setup** to add a buddy to the Buddy List.

■ The Buddy List Setup window appears.

4 Click the name of the group you want to add a buddy to.

5 Click **Add Buddy** to add a buddy to the group you selected.

How do I remove a person from my Buddy List?

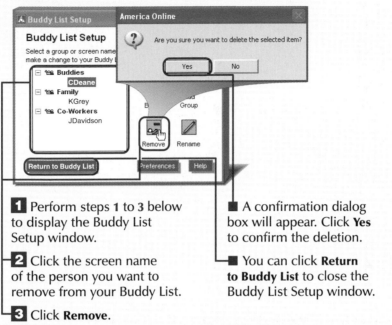

1 Perform steps **1** to **3** below to display the Buddy List Setup window.

2 Click the screen name of the person you want to remove from your Buddy List.

3 Click **Remove**.

■ A confirmation dialog box will appear. Click **Yes** to confirm the deletion.

■ You can click **Return to Buddy List** to close the Buddy List Setup window.

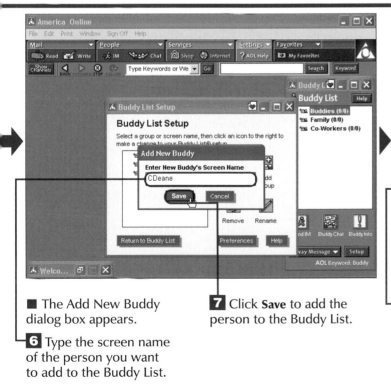

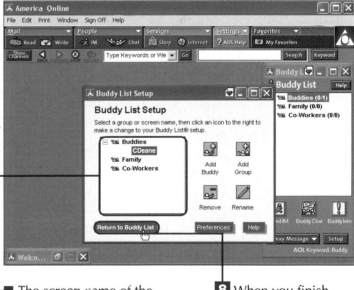

■ The Add New Buddy dialog box appears.

6 Type the screen name of the person you want to add to the Buddy List.

7 Click **Save** to add the person to the Buddy List.

■ The screen name of the person appears in this area.

■ You can repeat steps **4** to **7** for each person you want to add to the Buddy List.

8 When you finish adding buddies, click **Return to Buddy List** to close the Buddy List Setup window.

You can use the Buddy List to determine when your friends, family members and colleagues are online.

USING THE BUDDY LIST

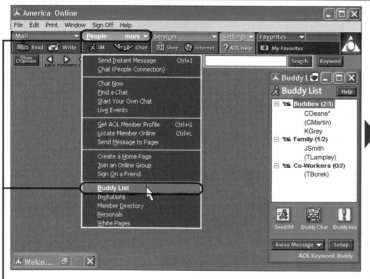

1 Click **People**.

2 Click **Buddy List**.

■ The Buddy List window appears.

Note: The Buddy List window may already be displayed on your screen. The window automatically appears each time you connect to AOL.

■ This area displays the name of each group in the Buddy List. The screen name of each buddy who is currently online appears below the appropriate group name.

■ The numbers in brackets beside each group name indicate how many buddies in the group are currently online and the total number of buddies in the group.

What can I do when I discover a buddy is online?

When a buddy is online, you can perform the following tasks to communicate with the buddy.

➢ If the buddy is in a public chat room, you can locate and join the buddy in the chat room. To locate a buddy, see page 90.

➢ You can send an instant message to start a private conversation with the buddy. To send an instant message, see page 84.

➢ You can use the Buddy Chat feature to create a private chat room and invite the buddy to join the chat. To use the Buddy Chat feature, see page 88.

Private Chat Room

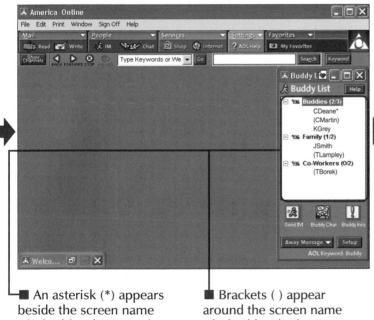

■ An asterisk (*) appears beside the screen name of a buddy who recently connected to AOL.

■ Brackets ( ) appear around the screen name of a buddy who has just disconnected from AOL.

3 To hide or display the buddies in a group, double-click the name of the group.

■ A plus sign (⊞) appears beside a group name when the buddies in the group are hidden.

■ When you finish working with the Buddy List, you can click ☒ to close the Buddy List window.

You can send an instant message to start a private conversation with a person in your Buddy List. The message will immediately appear on the other person's screen.

When sending an instant message, the person you want to receive the message must be online.

Sending instant messages is a great way to communicate with friends, family or colleagues without having to pay long-distance telephone charges.

SEND AN INSTANT MESSAGE

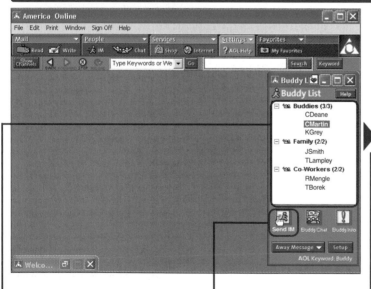

1 Click the screen name of the buddy you want to receive the instant message.

Note: If the Buddy List window is not displayed, perform steps 1 and 2 on page 80 to display the window.

2 Click **Send IM**.

■ The Send Instant Message window appears.

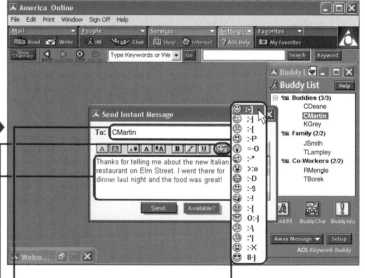

■ This area displays the screen name of the person you want to receive the instant message.

3 Click this area and type the message you want to send.

4 To add a graphical smiley to your message, click 🙂.

■ A list of graphical smileys appears.

5 Click the smiley you want to add to your message.

Can I send an instant message to a person who is not in my Buddy List?

Yes. You can send an instant message to any AOL member if you know their screen name.

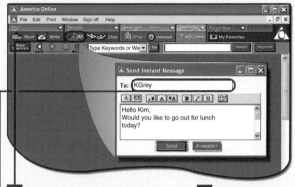

1 Click **IM** to display the Send Instant Message window.

2 Type the screen name of the person you want to receive the message.

3 Perform steps 3 to 7 below to compose and send the message.

Can I exchange instant messages with people who do not use AOL?

Yes. If you have a friend, colleague or family member who is not an AOL member, they can use the AOL Instant Messenger (AIM) software to exchange instant messages with you. The person can download the AOL Instant Messenger software free of charge from AOL's Web site at www.aol.com.

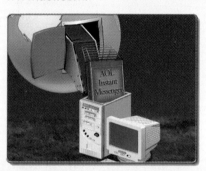

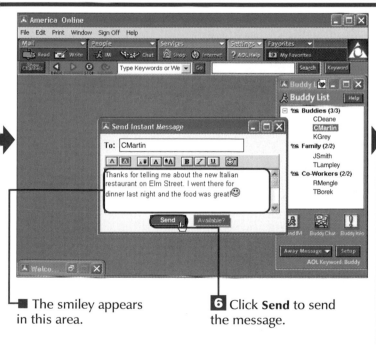

■ The smiley appears in this area.

6 Click **Send** to send the message.

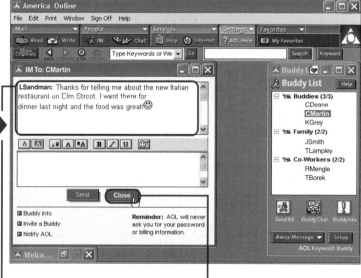

■ The IM To window appears.

■ This area displays your screen name and the message you sent.

■ You can repeat steps 3 to **6** for each message you want to send.

7 When you finish exchanging instant messages, click **Close** to close the window.

You can reply to an instant message you receive from another AOL member.

Any AOL member can send you an instant message if they know your screen name.

REPLY TO AN INSTANT MESSAGE

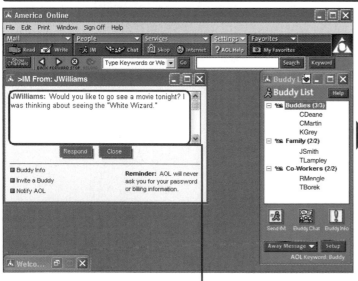

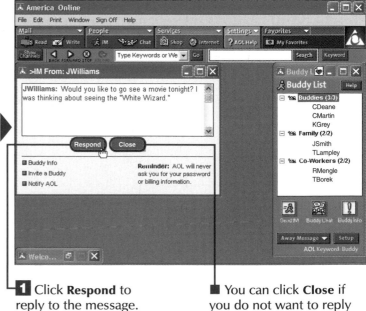

■ The IM From window appears on your screen when an AOL member sends you an instant message.

■ This area displays the screen name of the person who sent you the message and the contents of the message.

1 Click **Respond** to reply to the message.

■ You can click **Close** if you do not want to reply to the message.

86

What should I do if an AOL staff member asks for my password in an instant message?

An AOL staff member will never ask for your password or credit card information. If a member sends you an instant message claiming to be an AOL staff member and asks for this information, do not respond. You can click the box (■) beside **Notify AOL** at the bottom of the IM From window to report the person to AOL.

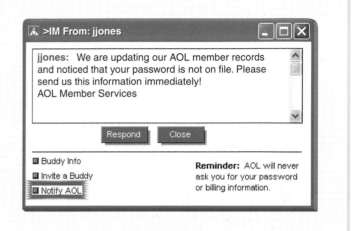

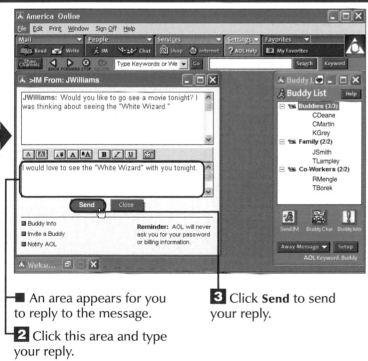

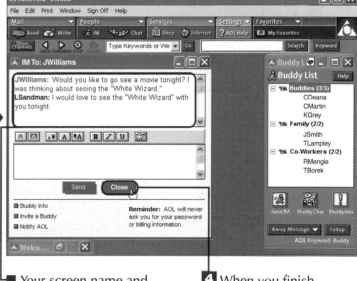

■ An area appears for you to reply to the message.

2 Click this area and type your reply.

3 Click **Send** to send your reply.

■ Your screen name and reply appear in this area.

■ You can repeat steps **2** and **3** for each reply you want to send.

4 When you finish exchanging instant messages, click **Close** to close the window.

Jim's Private Chat Room

You can use the Buddy Chat feature to quickly create a private chat room and invite people in your Buddy List to join the chat.

PRIVATE! Invited Guests — Only!

The buddies you want to chat with must be online.

Creating a Buddy Chat is ideal for having private discussions with friends, family members or colleagues.

CHAT WITH BUDDIES

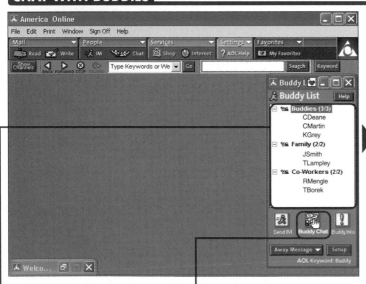

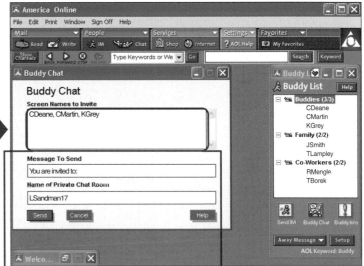

1 Click the name of the group that contains the buddies you want to invite to the Buddy Chat.

■ To invite an individual buddy to a Buddy Chat, click the screen name of the buddy.

Note: If the Buddy List window is not displayed, perform steps 1 and 2 on page 80 to display the window.

2 Click **Buddy Chat**.

■ The Buddy Chat window appears.

■ This area displays the screen name of each buddy you will invite to the Buddy Chat.

■ To remove the screen name of a buddy you do not want to invite, drag the mouse I over the screen name to highlight the name and then press the Delete key.

How do I join a Buddy Chat?

When a member invites you to a Buddy Chat, the
Invitation from window appears on your screen.

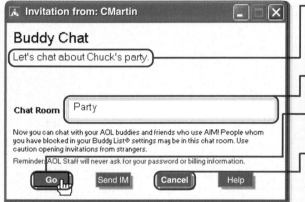

■ This area displays a
message from the member
who invited you to the
Buddy Chat.

■ This area displays the
name of the Buddy Chat.

1 Click **Go** to join the
Buddy Chat.

■ You can click **Cancel** to
close the Invitation from
window without joining
the Buddy Chat.

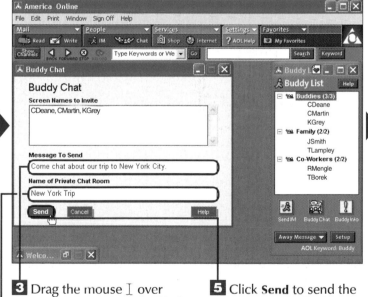

3 Drag the mouse I over
the text in this area to highlight
the text and then type a
message for the buddies you
are inviting to the Buddy Chat.

4 Double-click this area
and then type a name for
the Buddy Chat.

5 Click **Send** to send the
invitation to the buddies
you are inviting and go
to your Buddy Chat.

■ A window for the Buddy
Chat appears.

■ When a buddy joins the
chat, the buddy's screen
name appears in this area.
For information about
joining a Buddy Chat,
see the top of this page.

■ This area will display
the ongoing conversation
in the Buddy Chat. To
send a comment, see
page 100.

6 When you want to
leave the Buddy Chat,
click ⊠ to close the
window.

LOCATE A BUDDY

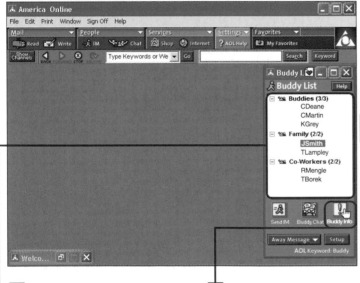

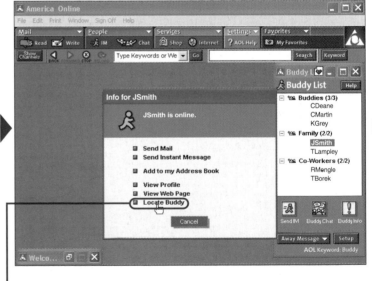

1 Click the screen name of the buddy you want to locate.

Note: If the Buddy List window is not displayed, perform steps 1 and 2 on page 80 to display the window.

2 Click **Buddy Info**.

■ The Info for dialog box appears.

3 Click **Locate Buddy** to locate the buddy.

■ The Locate window appears.

How can I locate an AOL member who is not in my Buddy List?

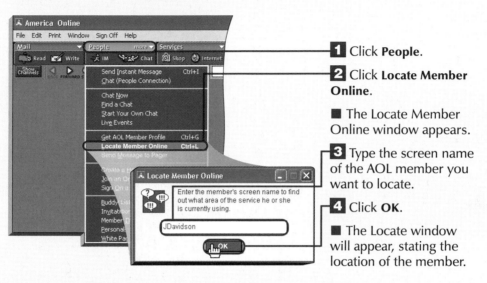

1 Click **People**.

2 Click **Locate Member Online**.

■ The Locate Member Online window appears.

3 Type the screen name of the AOL member you want to locate.

4 Click **OK**.

■ The Locate window will appear, stating the location of the member.

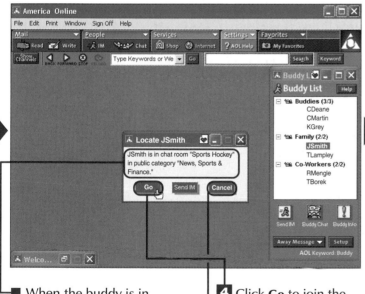

■ When the buddy is in a public chat room, the name of the chat room appears in this area.

Note: A different message appears if the buddy is in a private chat room, is not in a chat room or is not currently online.

4 Click **Go** to join the buddy in the public chat room.

Note: The Go button is only available if the buddy is in a public chat room.

■ If you do not want to join the public chat room, click **Cancel**.

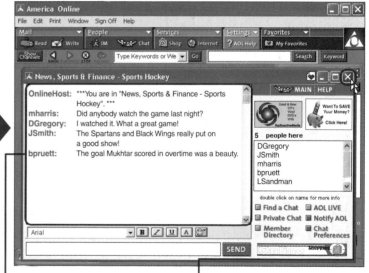

■ The chat room where the buddy is located appears on your screen.

■ This area displays the ongoing conversation.

Note: For information about using chat rooms, see pages 100 to 107.

5 When you want to leave the chat room, click ☒ to close the window.

You can turn on an away message to let other AOL members know that you are not available to receive instant messages.

AWAY MESSAGE:

At Lunch

I have stepped out to lunch.

I have stepped out to lunch.

Turning on an away message is useful when you will be away from your computer or when you want to use AOL without being interrupted by instant messages.

TURN ON AN AWAY MESSAGE

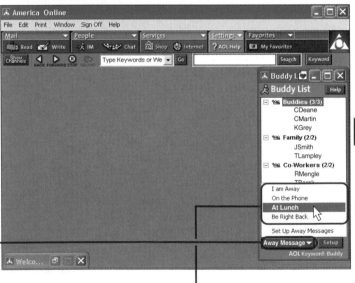

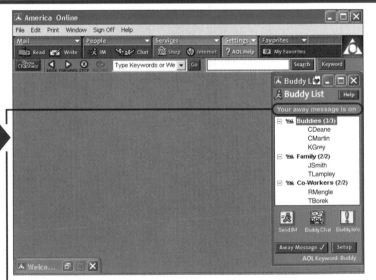

1 Click **Away Message**. A menu appears.

*Note: If the Buddy List window is not displayed, perform steps **1** and **2** on page 80 to display the window.*

2 Click the away message you want to use.

■ This message appears when an away message is turned on.

■ When a member sends you an instant message, the away message you selected will appear on their screen.

How can I quickly determine if a buddy has turned on an away message?

When a person you have added to your Buddy List turns on an away message, a notepad icon () appears beside the person's screen name in your Buddy List.

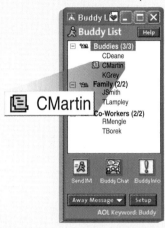

Will AOL ever automatically notify people when I am away from my computer?

Yes. When you do not use your computer for a period of time, AOL will automatically turn on an idle message. If a member sends you an instant message, the idle message will appear on their screen, letting them know you are online but may be away from AOL. The next time you use your keyboard or mouse, AOL will automatically turn off the idle message.

KGrey is online but may be away from AOL right now.

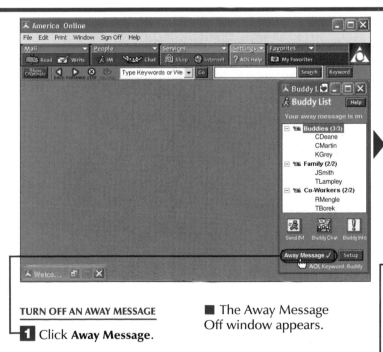

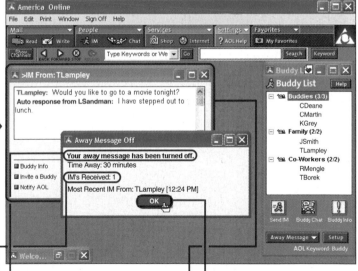

TURN OFF AN AWAY MESSAGE

1 Click **Away Message**.

■ The Away Message Off window appears.

■ This message indicates that the away message has been turned off.

■ This area displays the number of instant messages you received while the away message was turned on.

2 Click **OK** to close the Away Message Off window.

■ Any instant messages you received while the away message was turned on appear on your screen.

You can choose a buddy icon you want other AOL members to see while exchanging instant messages with you.

Choosing a buddy icon allows you to personalize your instant messages.

AOL offers more than 180 different buddy icons for you to choose from.

CHOOSE A BUDDY ICON

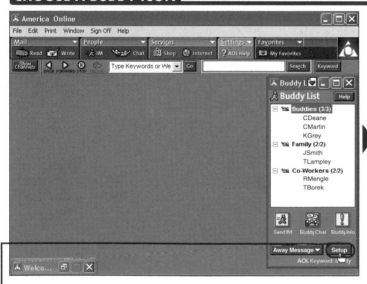

1 Click **Setup** to select a buddy icon.

Note: If the Buddy List window is not displayed, perform steps 1 and 2 on page 80 to display the window.

■ The Buddy List Setup window appears.

2 Click **Preferences**.

Where will the buddy icon I choose appear?

Instant Message Window

When you exchange instant messages with an AOL member, your buddy icon will appear at the bottom of the instant message window.

Buddy List

Once you exchange instant messages with an AOL member who has added you to their Buddy List, a miniature version of your buddy icon will appear beside your screen name in the member's Buddy List.

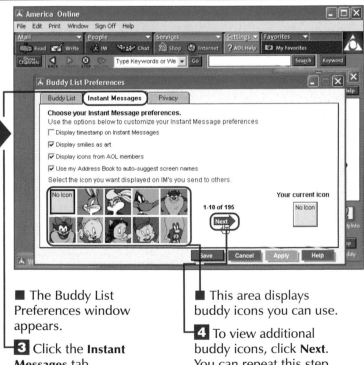

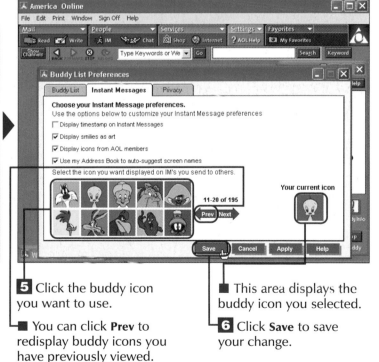

■ The Buddy List Preferences window appears.

3 Click the **Instant Messages** tab.

■ This area displays buddy icons you can use.

4 To view additional buddy icons, click **Next**. You can repeat this step until the buddy icon you want to use appears.

5 Click the buddy icon you want to use.

■ You can click **Prev** to redisplay buddy icons you have previously viewed.

■ This area displays the buddy icon you selected.

6 Click **Save** to save your change.

CHAPTER 7

CHAT WITH AOL MEMBERS

Are you interested in having online conversations with other AOL members? Read this chapter to learn how to join a chat room and create a private chat room.

You can find a chat room of interest to you. Chat rooms allow you to have online conversations with other AOL members.

AOL organizes chat rooms into categories such as Friends, Life and Romance.

Chat rooms provide a great way to meet other AOL members.

FIND A CHAT ROOM

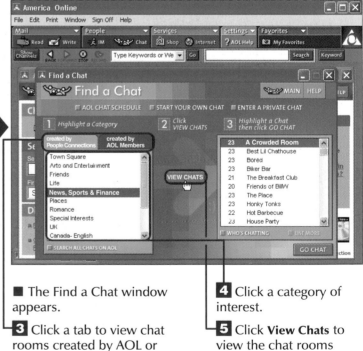

1 Click **Chat**.

■ The AOL People Connection window appears.

2 Click **Find a Chat**.

■ The Find a Chat window appears.

3 Click a tab to view chat rooms created by AOL or chat rooms created by AOL members.

4 Click a category of interest.

5 Click **View Chats** to view the chat rooms available in the category you selected.

What types of chat rooms can I join?

People Connection Chat Rooms

People Connection chat rooms are created and named by AOL. All members can join these chat rooms.

AOL Members Chat Rooms

AOL Members chat rooms are created and named by AOL members. All members can join these chat rooms.

Private Chat Rooms

Private chat rooms are created by AOL members. These chat rooms allow members to have private conversations. Only members who know the name of the private chat room can join. To join a private chat room, see the top of page 105.

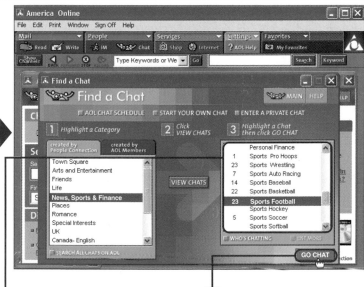

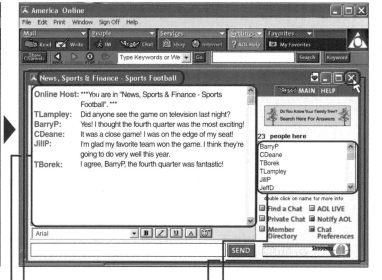

■ This area displays the chat rooms in the category you selected.

6 Click a chat room of interest.

7 Click **Go Chat** to join the chat room.

■ A window for the chat room appears.

■ This area displays the category and name of the chat room you selected.

■ This area displays the ongoing conversation in the chat room.

■ This area displays the screen name of each person in the chat room.

8 When you want to leave the chat room, click ☒ to close the window.

SEND A COMMENT

You can send a comment to a chat room to greet other chat members, ask questions or join the conversation.

SEND A COMMENT

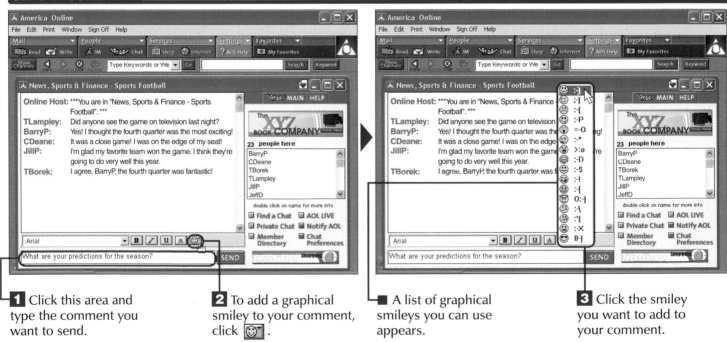

1 Click this area and type the comment you want to send.

2 To add a graphical smiley to your comment, click 😊.

■ A list of graphical smileys you can use appears.

3 Click the smiley you want to add to your comment.

What should I consider when sending comments to a chat room?

Avoid Including Private Information

Do not include private information about yourself in comments, such as your street address or telephone number. Everyone in the chat room will be able to see the comments you send.

Avoid Shouting

A COMMENT WRITTEN IN CAPITAL LETTERS IS ANNOYING AND DIFFICULT TO READ. THIS IS CALLED SHOUTING. Always use upper and lower case letters when typing comments.

Do Not Give Out Your Password

An AOL staff member will never ask for your password. To keep your AOL account secure, you should never give your password to anyone.

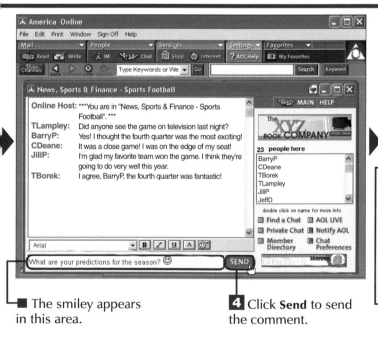

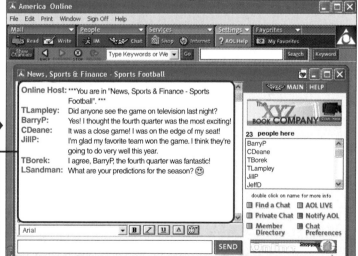

■ The smiley appears in this area.

4 Click **Send** to send the comment.

■ The comment appears in this area.

■ Everyone in the chat room can see the comment you sent.

You can view information about another member in a chat room, such as the person's name, location, hobbies and occupation.

If you want to create a member profile that other people in a chat room will be able to view, see page 146.

VIEW A MEMBER PROFILE

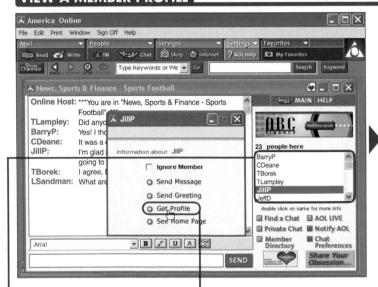

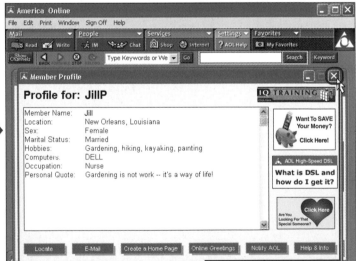

■ This area displays the screen name of each person in the chat room.

1 Double-click the screen name of the person whose profile you want to view.

■ A window appears, displaying a list of options.

2 Click **Get Profile**.

■ The Member Profile window appears, displaying information about the member.

*Note: A dialog box appears if no profile exists for the member. Click **OK** to close the dialog box.*

3 When you finish viewing the information, click ✕ to close the window.

You can ignore a chat member so their comments do not appear on your screen. This is a good way to remove conversation that does not interest you.

Although you will no longer see comments from a member you ignore, other people in the chat room will continue to see the member's comments.

IGNORE A CHAT MEMBER

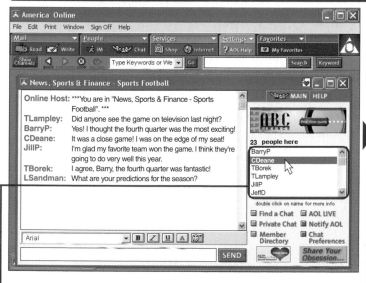

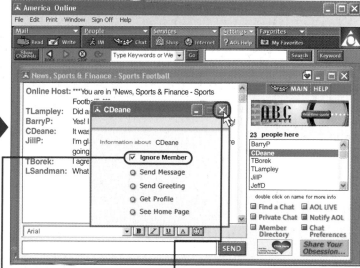

■ This area displays the screen name of each person in the chat room.

1 Double-click the screen name of the person whose comments you no longer want to see.

■ A window appears, displaying a list of options.

2 Click **Ignore Member** (☐ changes to ✔).

3 Click ✖ to close the window.

■ If you no longer want to ignore a member, repeat steps **1** to **3** (✔ changes to ☐ in step **2**).

You can create your own private chat room. This is ideal for having private discussions with colleagues, friends or family members.

Only people who know the name of your private chat room will be able to join the chat room.

CREATE A PRIVATE CHAT ROOM

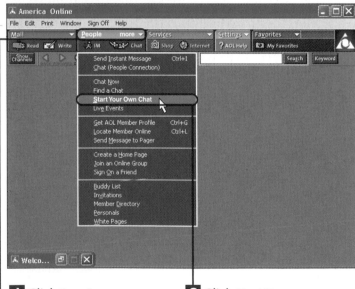

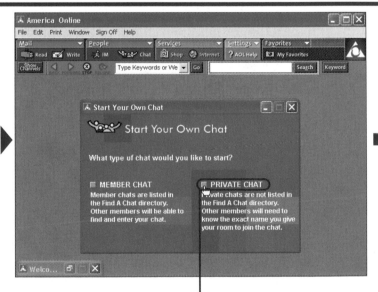

1 Click **People**.

2 Click **Start Your Own Chat**.

■ The Start Your Own Chat window appears.

3 Click the box (■) beside **Private Chat** to create a private chat room.

How do I join a private chat room?

You must know the exact name of the private chat room you want to join. AOL does not provide a list of private chat rooms. To join a private chat room, perform steps **1** to **5** below, except type the name of the chat room you want to join in step **4**.

Sorry, there are no private listings.

Is there another way to create a private chat room?

Yes. You can use AOL's Buddy Chat feature to quickly create a private chat room and invite people in your Buddy List to join the private chat. To create a private chat room using the Buddy Chat feature, see page 88.

PRIVATE!
Invited Buddies
Only!

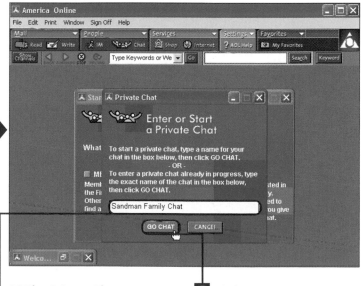

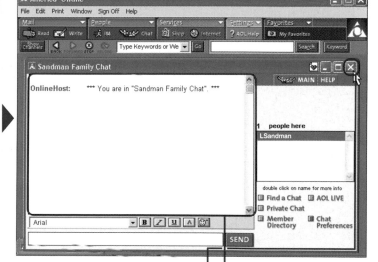

■ The Private Chat window appears.

4 Type a name for the private chat room you want to create.

5 Click **Go Chat** to go to your private chat room.

■ A window for the private chat room appears.

■ Other people can now join the private chat room. For information about joining a private chat room, see the top of this page.

■ This area will display the ongoing conversation in the private chat room.

6 When you want to leave the private chat room, click ✕ to close the window.

SEND AN INSTANT MESSAGE

When in a chat room, you can send an instant message to start a private conversation with another AOL member. The message will immediately appear on the other person's screen.

Have you ever visited Hawaii before?

Send Message

When you send an instant message, only the person you send the message to will see the message.

SEND AN INSTANT MESSAGE

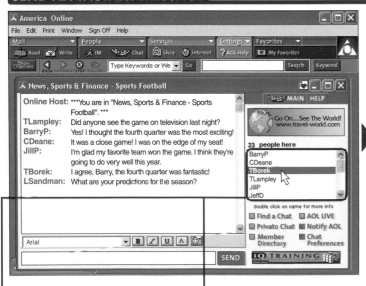

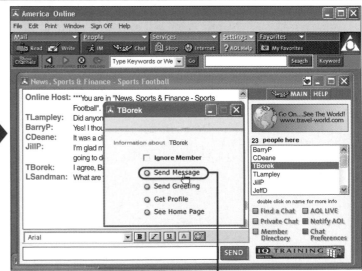

■ This area displays the screen name of each person in the chat room.

1 Double-click the screen name of the person you want to send an instant message to.

■ A window appears, displaying a list of options.

2 Click **Send Message** to send the person an instant message.

How do I reply to an instant message that another AOL member sends me?

When an AOL member sends you an instant message, the message will immediately appear on your screen. Any member can send you an instant message if they know your screen name.

If a member sends you an instant message claiming to be an AOL staff member and asks for your password or credit card number, do not give out this information. An AOL staff member will never ask for this information.

■ Click **Respond** to reply to the message.

■ Click **Close** if you do not want to reply to the message.

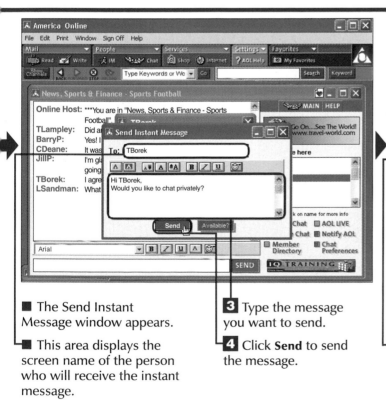

■ The Send Instant Message window appears.

■ This area displays the screen name of the person who will receive the instant message.

3 Type the message you want to send.

4 Click **Send** to send the message.

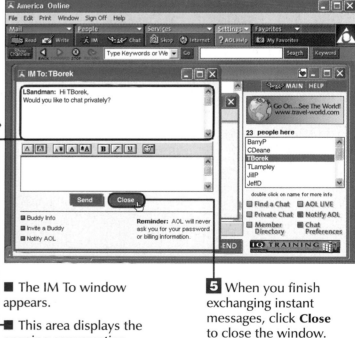

■ The IM To window appears.

■ This area displays the ongoing conversation.

■ You can repeat steps **3** and **4** for each message you want to send.

5 When you finish exchanging instant messages, click **Close** to close the window.

CHAPTER 8

ATTEND LIVE EVENTS

Would you like to meet your favorite celebrity online? Read this chapter to find out how to attend a live event and exchange questions and comments with the featured guest.

AOL offers live, interactive events where you can exchange questions and comments with special guests, including athletes, movie stars, musicians, politicians and writers.

AOL LIVE EVENTS

March 1	"Melting" Author Steve White
March 1	Football Legend Kevin Cooper
March 2	Soccer Ace Todd Webb
March 2	Comedian Bart Meuring
March 3	Romance Author Deb Campbell
March 3	Harvey Carroll

You can view a list of upcoming events on AOL so you can plan ahead to meet your favorite celebrities.

VIEW AOL LIVE EVENTS

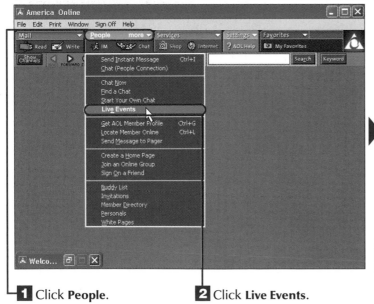

1 Click **People**.

2 Click **Live Events**.

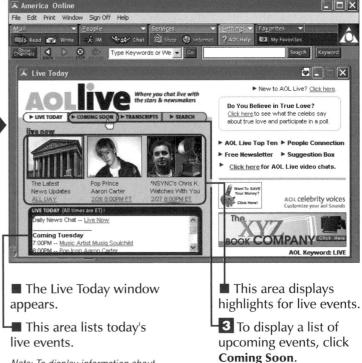

■ The Live Today window appears.

■ This area lists today's live events.

Note: To display information about one of today's live events, click the event and then skip to step 5.

■ This area displays highlights for live events.

3 To display a list of upcoming events, click **Coming Soon**.

How can I make sure I will not miss an upcoming live event?

You can subscribe to The LiveGuide newsletter to find out about upcoming live celebrity and expert guest appearances. The newsletter also contains interesting quotes from guests who have recently appeared on an AOL live event. AOL delivers the newsletter free of charge to your online mailbox every Monday.

Use the keyword **aol live newsletter** to display the AOL area that allows you to subscribe to the newsletter. For information about using keywords, see page 24.

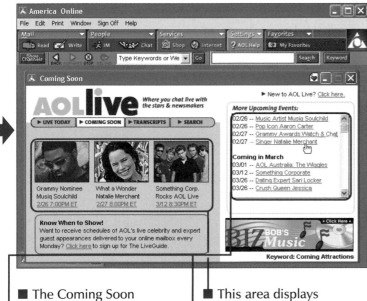

■ The Coming Soon window appears.

■ This area lists the date and topic for each upcoming live event.

■ This area displays highlights for upcoming live events.

4 Click an event of interest.

■ A window appears, displaying a description of the event you selected.

5 When you finish viewing the information, click ⊠ to close the window.

You can enter an auditorium to attend a live event. An auditorium has rows of people with a host and featured guest on stage.

When you attend a live event, AOL "seats" you in a row. Each row holds between 4 and 16 members.

ATTEND A LIVE EVENT

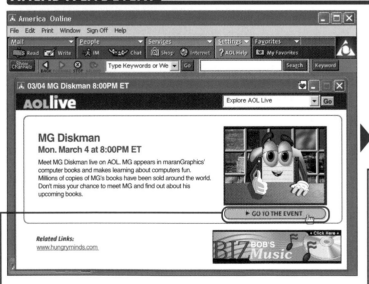

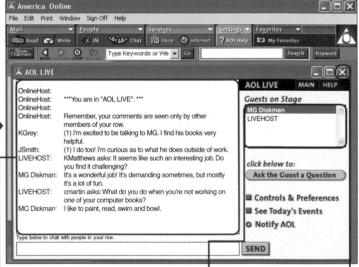

1 When viewing information about a live event that is currently in progress, click **Go To The Event** to attend the event.

Note: To view information about a live event, see page 110.

■ A window for the live event appears.

■ This area displays the ongoing conversation.

■ You can see the text typed by the host, guest(s) and members in your row. Comments typed by row members start with your row number in brackets.

■ This area displays the name(s) of the guest(s).

■ When you want to leave the live event, click ☒ to close the window.

TURN ROW CHAT OFF

You can ignore messages sent by other members in your row so their comments do not appear on your screen. This allows you to view only the text typed by the host and guest.

Turning off the row chat feature allows you to remove distracting conversation so you can concentrate on the live event.

TURN ROW CHAT OFF

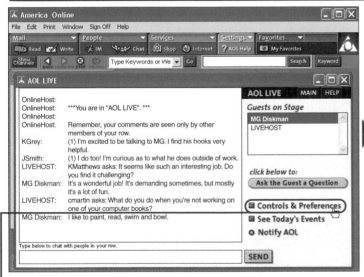

1 Click **Controls & Preferences**.

■ The Controls & Preferences window appears.

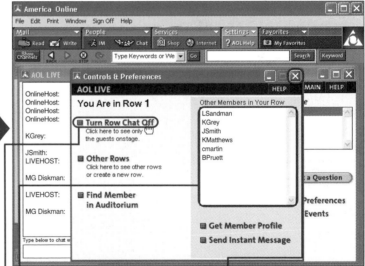

■ This area lists all the members in your row.

2 Click **Turn Row Chat Off** to ignore the messages sent by your row members (**Turn Row Chat Off** changes to **Turn Row Chat On**).

3 Click ☒ to close the window.

Note: To once again display the messages sent by your row members, repeat steps **1** to **3**, selecting **Turn Row Chat On** in step **2**.

SEND A MESSAGE

> While attending a live event, you can exchange messages with other members in your row.

When you attend a live event, AOL "seats" you in a row. Each row holds between 4 and 16 members. Only members in your row will see messages you send.

SEND A MESSAGE TO OTHER ROW MEMBERS

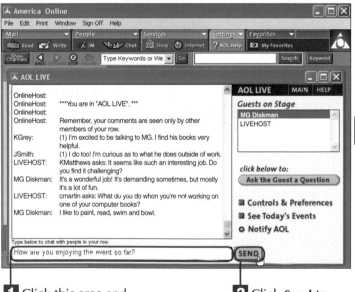

1 Click this area and type the message you want to send.

2 Click **Send** to send the message.

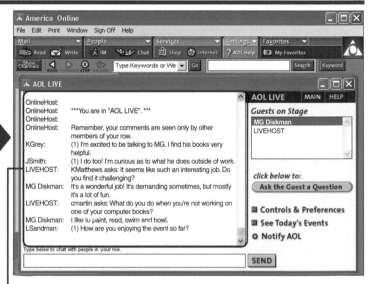

■ The message you sent appears in this area. The message starts with your row number in brackets.

You can send a question or comment to a featured guest at a live event.

Questions and comments the guest responds to will be seen by everyone in the auditorium.

SEND A MESSAGE TO THE GUEST

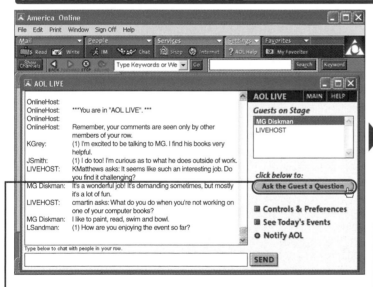

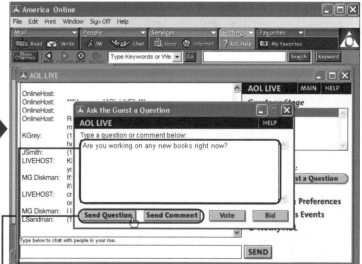

1 Click **Ask the Guest a Question**.

■ The Ask the Guest a Question window appears.

2 Type your question or comment.

3 Click **Send Question** or **Send Comment** to send your question or comment.

■ A dialog box will appear, confirming that your message was received. Click **OK** to close the dialog box.

SEARCH AOL LIVE EVENT TRANSCRIPTS

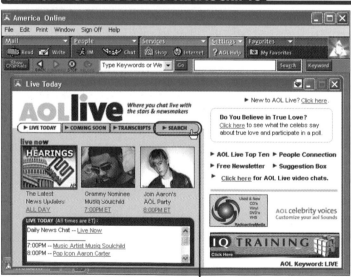

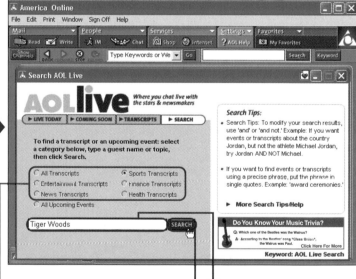

1 Perform steps **1** and **2** on page 110 to display the Live Today window.

2 Click **Search** to search for a transcript of a live event.

■ The Search AOL Live window appears.

3 Click a category to specify the type of event transcript you want to find (○ changes to ⊙).

*Note: If you do not know which category contains the event transcript you want to find, select **All Transcripts**.*

4 Click this area and then type a name, topic or date you want to find.

5 Click **Search** to start the search.

What celebrities have appeared on AOL?

Britney Spears

Madonna

Tiger Woods

Michael Jordan

Arnold Schwarzenegger

Christopher Reeve

Rosie O'Donnell

J.K. Rowling

What topics have appeared on AOL?

September 11 Terrorist Attacks

War on Terrorism

State of the Union Address

Elian Gonzales Coverage

Oscars Coverage

American Music Awards

Teen Choice Awards

"Survivor" Television Show

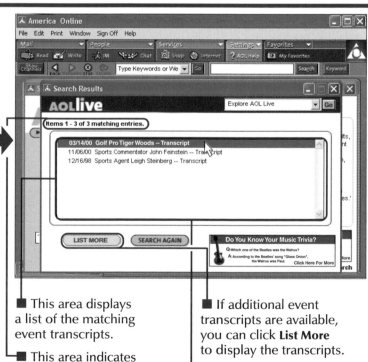

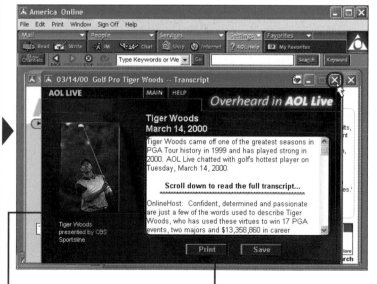

■ This area displays a list of the matching event transcripts.

■ This area indicates the number of matching transcripts displayed and the total number of matching transcripts.

■ If additional event transcripts are available, you can click **List More** to display the transcripts.

6 Double-click an event transcript of interest.

■ A window appears, displaying information about the event.

■ This area displays the transcript of the event.

7 When you finish reviewing the information, click **X** to close the window.

CHAPTER 9

USING MESSAGE BOARDS

Are you interested in communicating with other AOL members who share your interests? In this chapter you will learn how to read and add messages to message boards.

REPLY

Try layering your clothing under your ski jacket and pants. Taking warm-up breaks inside will also help.
Good Luck!
Brian Edwards

I am looking for suggestions on how to stay warm.

ORIGINAL MESSAGE

I always get really co... when I ski. I am looki... for suggestions on how to stay warm.
Thanks

Dan Duncan

INTRODUCTION TO MESSAGE BOARDS

Message boards allow you to exchange information with other AOL members who share your interests.

AOL Members Only

Each message board discusses information about a specific topic. AOL offers message boards for topics such as books, movies, parenting, pets and travel destinations. You can find message boards in most AOL areas.

MESSAGE BOARD GUIDELINES

Read Messages

Read the messages in a message board for a few days before sending a message. This is a great way to learn how people in the message board communicate and prevents you from sending information others have already read.

Check Content

Check your messages for spelling, grammar and clarity. Also, make sure readers will not misinterpret your messages. For example, a reader may not realize a statement is meant to be sarcastic.

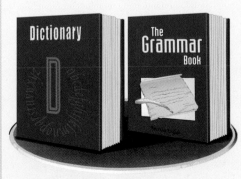

Avoid Offensive Language

Avoid using insulting, obscene or abusive language in your messages. People of all ages and backgrounds can read messages you send.

My @#!#? car broke down again. Does anyone know a good mechanic in the NY area?

Avoid Chain Letters or Advertisements

Do not send chain letters or advertisements to message boards. AOL offers a few message boards designed specifically for advertisements. You should send advertisements only to these message boards.

Avoid Shouting

DO NOT TYPE MESSAGES IN ALL CAPITAL LETTERS. This is called shouting and will annoy readers and make your messages more difficult to read. Always use upper and lower case letters when typing messages.

Avoid Cross-posting

Do not send a single message to several message boards. This is called cross-posting. Send one message to the most appropriate message board to ensure the people most interested in your comments will see your message.

Avoid Including Private Information

Do not include private information about yourself, such as your phone number or address. You can always send this information to individual members by e-mail, if needed.

Send Meaningful Replies

You should reply to a message only when you have something important to say. A reply such as "Me too" or "I agree" is not very informative.

Read Guidelines

A message board may contain guidelines that you should read before sending a message to the board. Guidelines can include rules for sending messages and answers to frequently asked questions. The guidelines for a message board are often named Standards, Posting Standards or Community Standards.

You can read the messages in a message board of interest to learn the opinions and ideas of other AOL members.

Most AOL areas have message boards that discuss information related to the area.

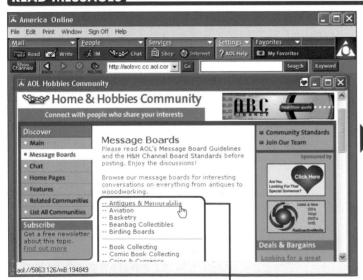

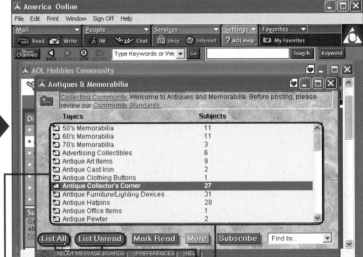

1 Locate a message board of interest.

*Note: In this example, we used the keyword **hobbies community** to locate message boards that discuss hobbies. For information about using keywords, see page 24.*

2 Click the message board of interest.

■ A window appears, displaying the message boards and the number of subjects in each board. Message boards display the 🗔 symbol.

Note: Folders display the 📁 symbol. You can double-click a folder to display the message boards in the folder.

3 Click a message board of interest.

4 Click **List All** to list all the subjects in the message board.

■ To list only the subjects you have not previously read, click **List Unread**.

How can I quickly find messages of interest?

You can use AOL's Quick Search feature to search for messages containing a specific word or phrase.

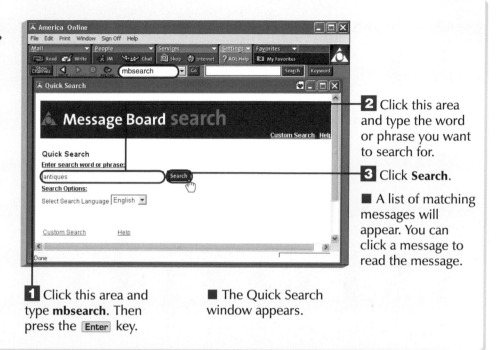

2 Click this area and type the word or phrase you want to search for.

3 Click **Search**.

■ A list of matching messages will appear. You can click a message to read the message.

1 Click this area and type **mbsearch**. Then press the Enter key.

■ The Quick Search window appears.

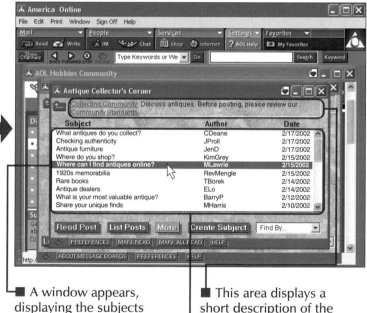

■ A window appears, displaying the subjects in the message board you selected.

Note: Each subject can have one or more messages. A subject can include an initial question and the replies from other readers.

■ This area displays a short description of the message board.

5 Double-click a subject of interest.

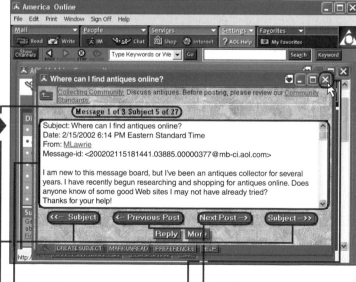

■ A window appears, displaying the contents of the first message in the subject.

■ This area indicates which message and subject you are viewing.

6 Click **<<—Subject** or **Subject—>>** to display the previous or next subject.

■ Click **<—Previous Post** or **Next Post—>** to display the previous or next message in the current subject.

7 When you finish reading messages, click **X** to close the window.

You can produce a paper copy of the message displayed on your screen. Printing a message is useful when the message contains information you want to keep.

A printed message displays the date, your screen name and the page number at the bottom of each page.

PRINT A MESSAGE

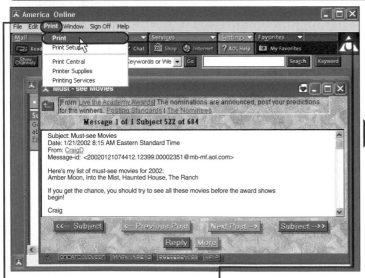

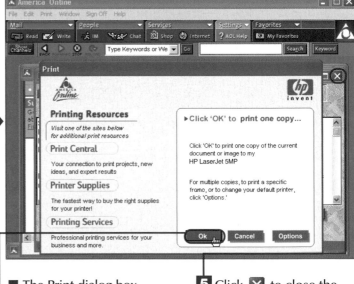

1 Display the contents of the message you want to print. To display the contents of a message, see page 122.

2 Click **Print**.

3 Click **Print** to print the message.

■ The Print dialog box appears.

4 Click **Ok** to print the message.

5 Click ☒ to close the window that displays the contents of the message.

When you finish reading the messages of interest in a message board, you can mark all the messages as read.

The next time you visit a message board you marked as read, you can list the unread messages in the board to display only the messages that were added since you last visited the message board. To list unread messages, see page 122.

MARK ALL MESSAGES AS READ

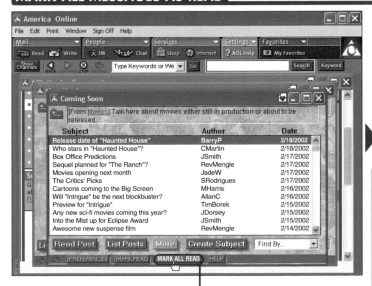

1 Display the list of subjects in the message board that you want to mark as read. To display a list of subjects in a message board, see page 122.

2 Click **Mark All Read** to mark all the messages in the message board as read.

■ A confirmation dialog box appears.

3 Click **OK** to close the dialog box.

You can add, or post, a new message to a message board to ask a question, express an opinion or supply new information.

Each message board discusses information about a specific topic. Make sure you add a message to the appropriate message board. Adding an unrelated message, such as an advertisement, to a message board will annoy other members.

ADD A MESSAGE

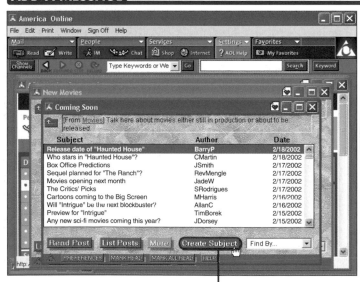

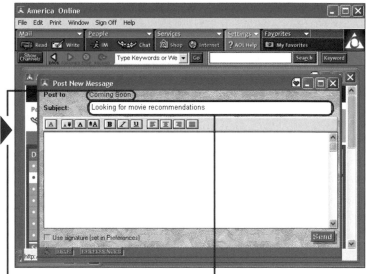

1 Display the list of subjects in the message board you want to add a message to. To display a list of subjects in a message board, see page 122.

2 Click **Create Subject** to add a message to the message board.

■ The Post New Message window appears.

■ The AOL software fills in the name of the message board for you.

3 Type the subject of the message. Make sure the subject clearly describes the contents of your message.

What symbols and abbreviations can I use in my messages?

Smileys

:) = Smile
;) = Wink
:D = Laugh
:(= Frown
:'(= Cry

Smileys

You can use special characters, called smileys, to express emotions in your messages. These characters resemble human faces if you turn them sideways.

Abbreviations

BTW = By The Way
FYI = For Your Information
GMTA = Great Minds Think Alike
IOW = In Other Words
LOL = Laughing Out Loud
WTG = Way To Go

Abbreviations

You can use abbreviations in your messages to save time typing.

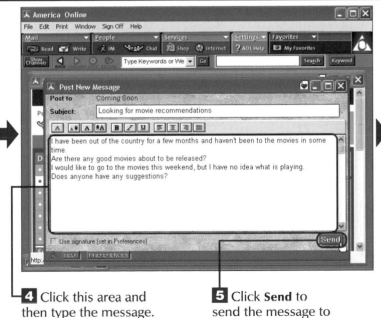

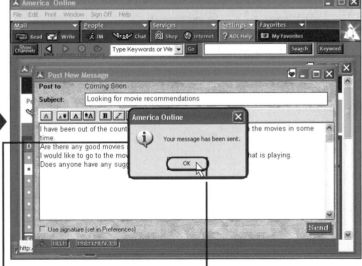

4 Click this area and then type the message. Make sure the message is clear, concise and does not contain spelling or grammar errors.

5 Click **Send** to send the message to the message board.

■ A dialog box appears, confirming the message was sent.

6 Click **OK** to close the dialog box.

You can reply to a message to answer a question, express an opinion or offer additional information.

REPLY

Try layering your clothing under your ski jacket and pants. Taking warm-up breaks inside will also help.
Good Luck!
Brian Edwards

I am looking for suggestions on how to stay warm.

ORIGINAL MESSAGE

I always get really cold when I ski. I am looking for suggestions on how to stay warm.
Thanks
Dan Duncan

You should reply to a message only when you have something important to say. A reply such as "Me too" or "I agree" is not very informative.

You can include all or part of the original message in your reply to help readers identify which message you are replying to. This is called quoting.

REPLY TO A MESSAGE

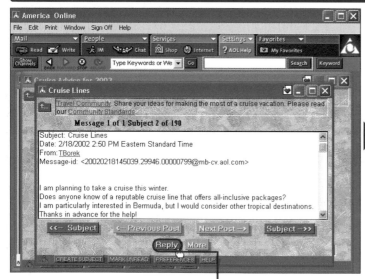

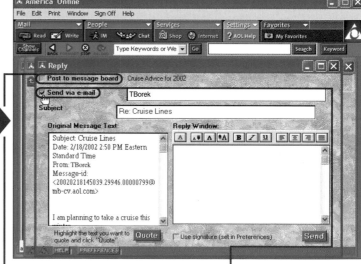

1 Display the contents of the message you want to reply to. To display the contents of a message, see page 122.

2 Click **Reply** to reply to the message.

■ The Reply window appears for you to compose the reply.

3 The AOL software will automatically send the reply to the message board. Click this option if you do not want to send the message to the message board (☑ changes to ☐).

4 Click this option if you want to send a private e-mail message to the author of the original message (☐ changes to ☑).

How can I reply to a message?

You can send a reply to the message board, to just the author of the original message, or to both.

Post to message board

Send a reply to the message board when your comments would be of interest to others reading the message board.

Send via e-mail

Send an e-mail message to just the author when your reply would not be of interest to others reading the message board or if you want to send a private response.

I cannot find a reply I sent to a message board. What is wrong?

It may take a while for the AOL software to process your reply. If your reply does not immediately appear on the message board, do not resend the reply. Try checking the message board again later to view your reply.

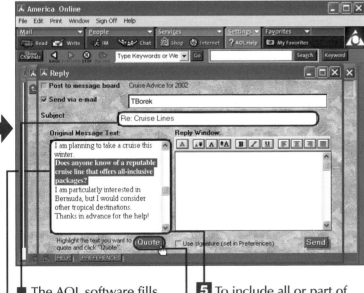

■ The AOL software fills in the subject, starting the subject with **Re:**.

■ This area displays the original message.

5 To include all or part of the original message in your reply, drag the mouse over the text you want to include until you highlight the text.

6 Click **Quote** to include the text in your reply.

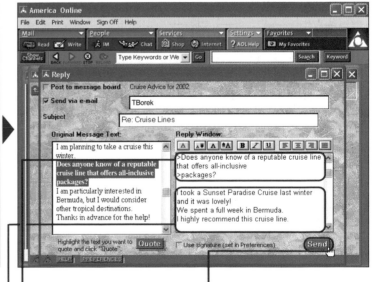

■ This area displays the text you included from the original message.

7 Type your reply.

8 Click **Send** to send your reply.

■ A dialog box will appear, confirming that the message was sent. Click **OK** to close the dialog box.

CHAPTER 10

CREATE AND JOIN GROUPS

Would you like to set up a group that discusses a topic of interest to you? In this chapter you will learn how to create a group, invite members to join your group and add messages to the group.

Any AOL member
over the age of 18
can create a group.

CREATE A GROUP

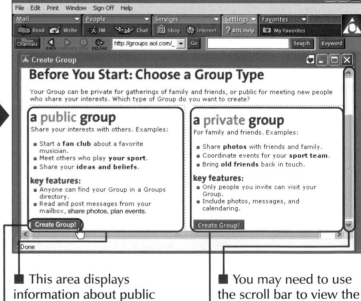

1 Click this area and type **Groups**. Then press the Enter key.

■ The My Groups window appears.

2 Click **Create Group!** to create a group.

■ The Create Group window appears.

■ This area displays information about public groups.

3 Click **Create Group!** in this area to create a public group.

■ You may need to use the scroll bar to view the Create Group! button.

■ This area displays information about private groups. For more information about private groups, see the top of page 133.

What is the difference between a public group and a private group?

Unlike a public group, a private group is not available for all AOL members to join. Only members who are invited can join a private group. Creating a private group is useful when you want to communicate privately with friends and family members. To create a private group, perform steps **1** to **3** below, selecting the **Create Group!** button below the information about private groups in step **3**. Then follow the instructions on your screen to finish creating the private group.

Where will the group name and description I specify for my group appear?

The name and description you specify for your group will appear in the Group Directory. The Group Directory is a list of all the available public groups. AOL members can search the Group Directory to find groups they want to join. To search for a group, see page 138.

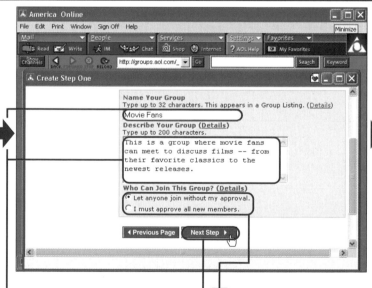

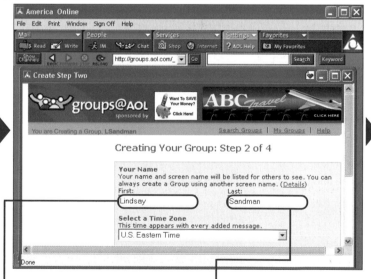

■ The Create Step One window appears.

4 Click this area and type a name for your group.

5 Click this area and type a description of your group.

6 Click the circle (○) beside an option to specify whether you want to approve new members before they can join your group (○ changes to ⦿).

7 Click **Next Step** to continue.

■ The Create Step Two window appears.

8 Click this area and type your first name.

9 Click this area and type your last name.

Note: Your name and screen name will be available for other members of the group to see.

CONTINUED

Members of the group will use the e-mail address you specify to send messages to the group.

CREATE A GROUP (CONTINUED)

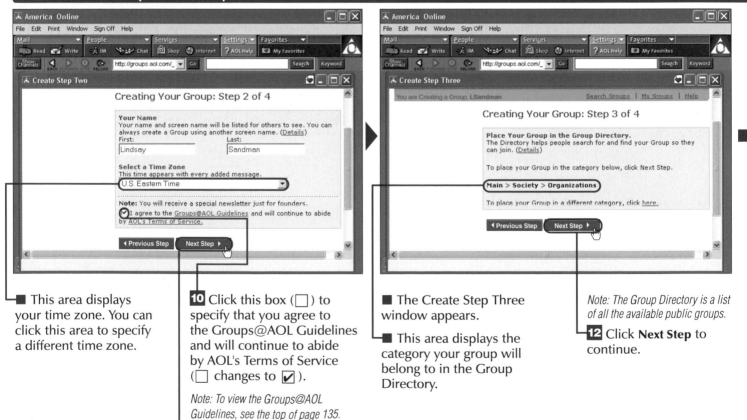

■ This area displays your time zone. You can click this area to specify a different time zone.

10 Click this box (☐) to specify that you agree to the Groups@AOL Guidelines and will continue to abide by AOL's Terms of Service (☐ changes to ☑).

Note: To view the Groups@AOL Guidelines, see the top of page 135.

11 Click **Next Step** to continue.

■ The Create Step Three window appears.

■ This area displays the category your group will belong to in the Group Directory.

Note: The Group Directory is a list of all the available public groups.

12 Click **Next Step** to continue.

How can I view the Groups@AOL Guidelines?

In the Create Step Two window, click the **Groups@AOL Guidelines** link to display the guidelines for creating a public group. You should read the guidelines carefully before performing step **10** below.

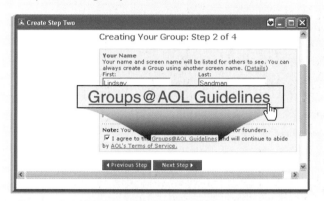

Where can I find more information about creating groups?

After you create a group, AOL will automatically send a newsletter to your online mailbox that contains information about the group and your responsibilities as the group's creator. You can also use the keyword **Groupfounders** to display an area where you can exchange ideas with other people who have created groups. For information about using keywords, see page 24.

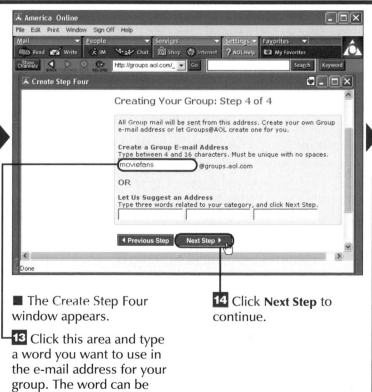

■ The Create Step Four window appears.

13 Click this area and type a word you want to use in the e-mail address for your group. The word can be between 4 and 16 characters, with no spaces.

14 Click **Next Step** to continue.

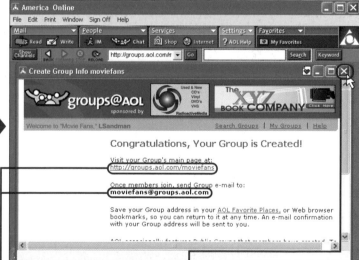

■ The Create Group Info window appears.

■ This area displays the address of your group's main page.

■ This area displays the e-mail address you specified for the group.

15 When you finish viewing the information about your group, click ✕ to close the Create Group Info window.

■ You can now invite members to join your group. To invite members to join your group, see page 136.

INVITE MEMBERS TO JOIN A GROUP

> Once you create a group, you can invite members to join the group.

Members you invite to join your group will have 60 days to join before the invitation expires.

INVITE MEMBERS TO JOIN A GROUP

1 Click this area and type **Groups**. Then press the **Enter** key.

■ The My Groups window appears.

■ This area displays the name of each group you have created.

Note: The area also displays the names of any groups you have joined. For information about joining a group, see the top of page 137.

2 Click the name of the group you want to invite members to join.

■ The Main Page window appears, displaying the main page for the group.

3 Click **Invite a friend** to invite members to join the group.

■ The Sending Invites window appears.

I have been invited to join a group. How do I join?

When someone invites you to join a group, you will receive an e-mail message that provides information about the group, such as the name of the group and a short description of the group.

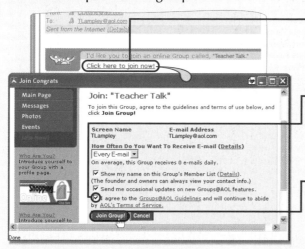

1 To join the group, click the **Click here to join now!** link in the e-mail message.

■ The Join Congrats window appears.

2 Click this box (☐) to specify that you agree to the Groups@AOL Guidelines and will continue to abide by AOL's Terms of Service (☐ changes to ☑).

3 Click **Join Group!**.

■ The Main Page window will appear, displaying a message congratulating you on becoming a member of the group.

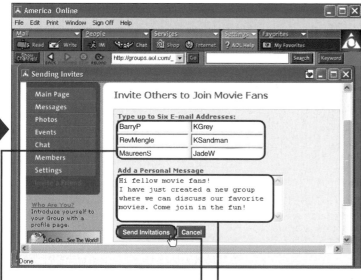

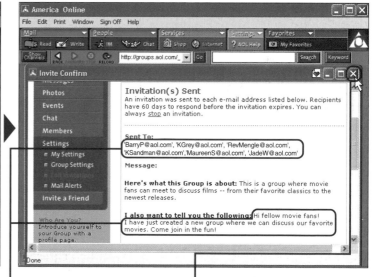

■ This area displays boxes where you can enter the screen names of up to six members you want to invite to join the group.

4 Click a box and then type the screen name of a member you want to invite. Repeat this step for each member you want to invite.

5 Click this area and type a personal message that you want to appear in the invitation.

6 Click **Send Invitations** to invite the members to join your group.

■ The Invite Confirm window appears.

■ This area displays the members you invited to join the group.

■ This area displays the personal message you included in the invitation.

■ You may need to use the scroll bar to view the entire invitation.

7 When you finish viewing the invitation, click ✕ to close the Invite Confirm window.

Once you find a group of interest, you can join the group.

SEARCH FOR A GROUP

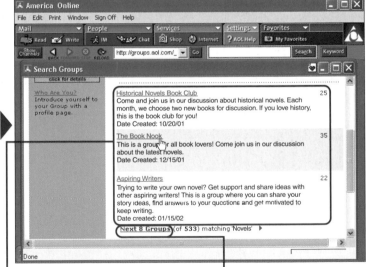

1 Click this area and type **Groups**. Then press the `Enter` key.

■ The My Groups window appears.

2 To find a group that discusses a topic of interest, click this area and type a word or phrase that describes the topic.

3 Click **Search** to start the search.

■ The Search Groups window appears, displaying a list of groups that match the word or phrase you specified and the number of members in each group.

4 Click a group of interest.

■ If the list of matching groups is more than one page long, you can click **Next** to view the next page of matching groups.

■ You may need to use the scroll bar to view the Next link.

Why do I have to ask permission to join some groups?

You must ask permission to join a group when the creator of the group has specified that they want to approve all new members.

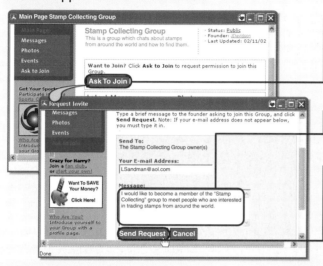

1 To ask permission to join a group, click the **Ask To Join** button.

■ The Request Invite window appears.

2 Click this area and type a message asking permission to join the group.

3 Click **Send Request** to send the message.

■ You will receive an e-mail message notifying you whether your request to join the group was approved or declined.

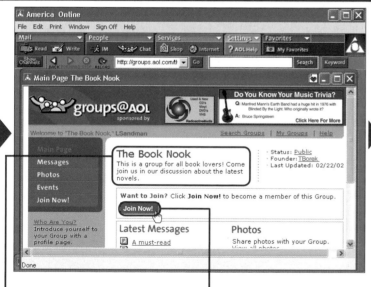

■ The Main Page window appears, displaying the main page for the group.

■ This area displays a short description of the group.

5 To join the group, click **Join Now!**.

Note: If the Ask To Join button appears instead of the Join Now! button, see the top of this page.

■ The Join Group window appears.

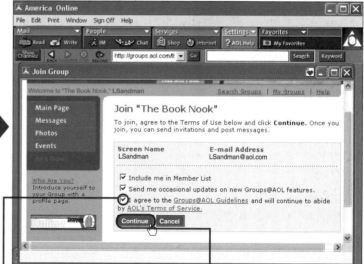

6 Click this box (☐) to specify that you agree to the Groups@AOL Guidelines and will continue to abide by AOL's Terms of Service (☐ changes to ☑).

7 Click **Continue** to join the group.

■ The Main Page window will reappear, displaying a message congratulating you on becoming a member of the group. You can click ☒ to close the window.

You can read the messages in a group to learn the opinions and ideas of other members of the group.

READ MESSAGES

1 Click this area and type **Groups**. Then press the Enter key.

■ The My Groups window appears.

■ This area displays the name of each group you have created or joined.

2 Click the name of the group you want to read the messages for.

■ The Main Page window appears, displaying the main page for the group.

■ This area displays the subjects of the latest messages sent to the group. To read one of these messages, click the subject of the message. Then skip to step **5**.

3 To view a list of all the messages in the group, click **View all messages**.

Note: If the View all messages link is not displayed, the group does not contain additional messages.

■ The Message List window appears.

Do I have to be a member of a group to read the messages in the group?

You do not have to be a member of a group to read the messages in the group. Reading the messages in a group before joining can help you decide if you want to become a member of the group. To read the messages in a group before joining, locate a group of interest and then perform steps **3** to **6** below. To locate a group, see page 138.

■ This area displays the subjects of the messages in the group and the number of messages in each subject.

■ If additional subjects are available, you can click **Next** to display the subjects.

4 Click a subject of interest.

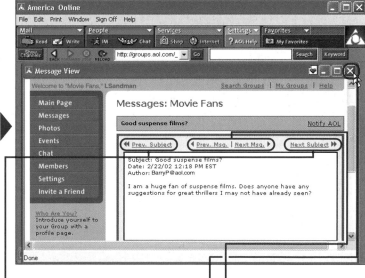

■ The Message View window appears, displaying the contents of the first message in the subject.

5 Click **Prev. Subject** or **Next Subject** to display the previous or next subject.

■ Click **Prev. Msg.** or **Next Msg.** to display the previous or next message in the current subject.

6 When you finish reading messages, click ☒ to close the Message View window.

ADD A MESSAGE

You can add a message to a group to ask a question, express an opinion or supply new information.

To add a message to a group, you must be a member of the group.

When you add a message to a group, AOL automatically sends the message to the online mailbox of each member of the group.

ADD A MESSAGE

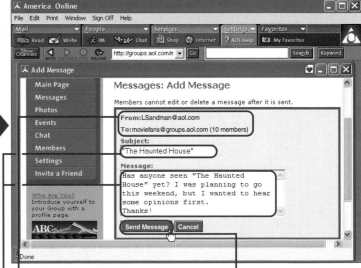

1 Display the main page for the group you want to add a message to. To display the main page for a group, perform steps **1** and **2** on page 140.

2 Click **Add Message** to add a message to the group.

■ The Add Message window appears.

■ AOL fills in your e-mail address and the e-mail address of the group for you.

3 Click this area and type a subject for your message.

4 Click this area and type your message.

5 Click **Send Message** to add the message to the group.

■ The Message Added window will appear, confirming that your message was added to the group. You can click ☒ to close the window.

REPLY TO A MESSAGE

You can reply to a message in a group to answer a question, express an opinion or offer additional information.

You can include the original message in your reply to help readers identify which message you are replying to.

To reply to a message in a group, you must be a member of the group.

When you reply to a message in a group, AOL automatically sends the reply to the online mailbox of each member of the group.

REPLY TO A MESSAGE

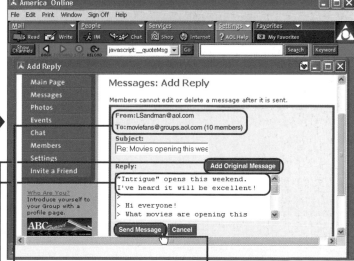

1 Display the contents of a message you want to reply to. To display the contents of a message, see page 140.

2 Click **Add Reply** to reply to the message.

■ The Add Reply window appears.

■ AOL fills in your e-mail address and the e-mail address of the group for you.

3 To include the original message in your reply, click **Add Original Message**.

4 Click this area and type your reply.

5 Click **Send Message** to add the reply to the group.

■ The Message Added window will appear, confirming that your message was added to the group. You can click ✕ to close the window.

CHAPTER 11

CUSTOMIZE AOL

Do you want to learn how to customize AOL to suit your needs? This chapter will teach you how to create a list of your favorite places on AOL, create a news profile to have news articles delivered to your online mailbox and create a stock portfolio to track your investments.

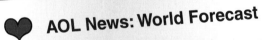

AOL News: World Forecast

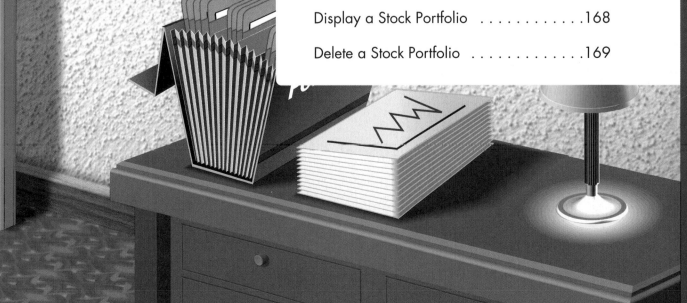

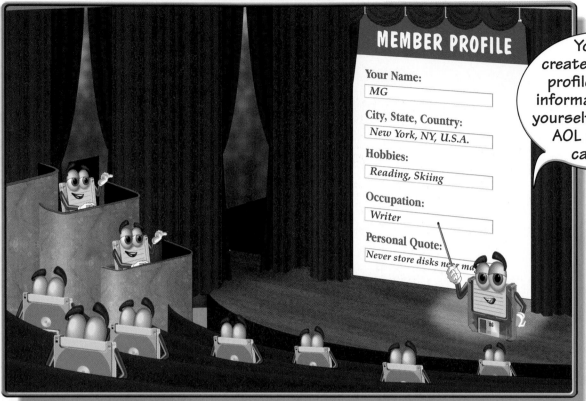

You can create a member profile to store information about yourself that other AOL members can view.

Do not include information in your member profile that you want to keep private, such as your full name, address or telephone number.

Creating a member profile is optional.

CREATE A MEMBER PROFILE

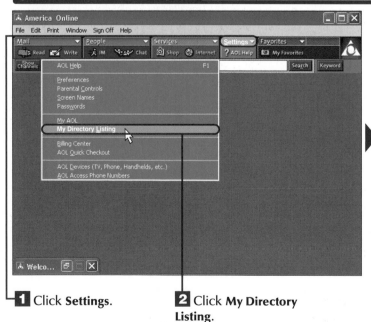

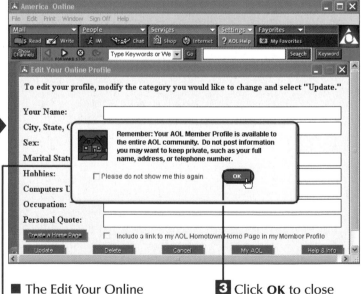

1 Click **Settings**.

2 Click **My Directory Listing**.

■ The Edit Your Online Profile window appears.

■ A dialog box also appears, stating that your member profile will be available to all AOL members.

3 Click **OK** to close the dialog box.

How can people view my member profile?

Member Directory

When you create a member profile, AOL automatically adds the profile to the Member Directory. Other AOL members can search the directory to find your profile based on your name, interests or other information. To search the Member Directory, see page 148.

Chat Rooms

While chatting, other AOL members in the chat room can view your member profile to learn more about you. To view a member profile while chatting, see page 102.

Can I change the information in my member profile?

You can edit your member profile to update the information in the profile. To edit your member profile, perform steps **1** to **7** below. If an area already contains text, drag the mouse I over the text before typing the new information.

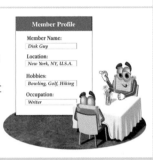

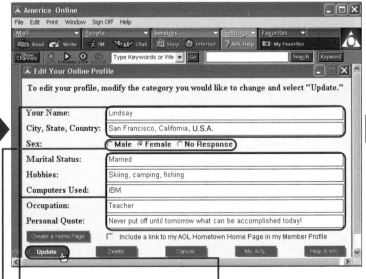

4 Click each area and type the appropriate information. You can leave areas blank if you wish.

5 Click an option to indicate whether you are male, female or do not want to respond (○ changes to ⦿).

6 Click **Update** when you finish entering the information.

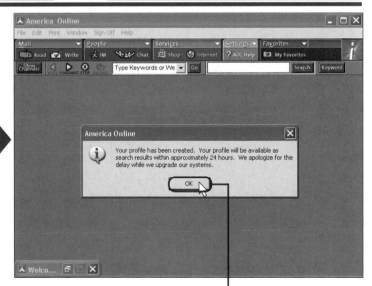

■ A confirmation dialog box appears, stating that your profile has been created.

7 Click **OK** to close the dialog box.

SEARCH THE MEMBER DIRECTORY

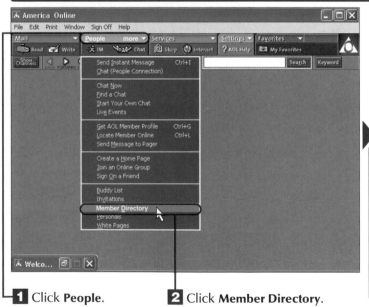

1 Click **People**.

2 Click **Member Directory**.

■ The Member Directory window appears.

3 Type the information you want to search for.

4 Click **Search** to start the search.

■ The Member Directory Search Results window appears.

Why would I search the Member Directory?

Searching the Member Directory allows you to determine the screen names of family members, friends and colleagues as well as AOL members who share your interests. Once you determine the screen name of an AOL member, you can use the screen name to send the person an e-mail message or an instant message.

Are all AOL members listed in the Member Directory?

No. Only AOL members who have created a member profile are listed in the Member Directory. If an AOL member has not created a member profile, you will not be able to find the person by searching the Member Directory. To create your member profile, see page 146.

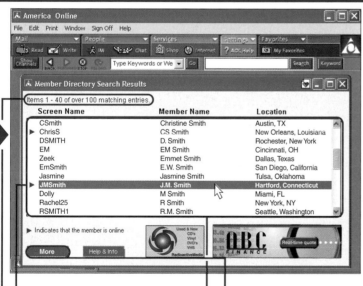

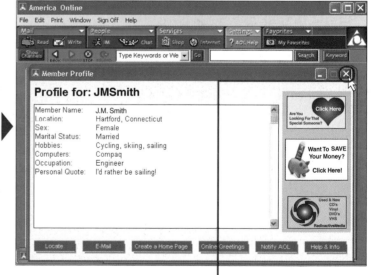

■ This area lists the members who match the information you entered. An arrow (▶) appears beside each member who is currently online.

■ This area indicates the number of members displayed and the total number of matching members.

5 To display additional members, click **More**.

6 To view the member profile for a member, double-click the member.

■ The Member Profile window appears, displaying information about the member.

7 When you finish viewing the information, click ✕ to close the window.

You can create a list of your favorite places on AOL so you can quickly return to those places.

Your list of favorite places can include AOL areas and Web pages.

1 Display the location you want to add to your list of favorite places.

2 Click the heart icon (♥) at the top of the window.

Note: If the window does not display a heart icon (♥), you cannot add the location to your list of favorite places.

■ The America Online dialog box appears.

3 Click **Add to Favorites** to add the location to your list of favorite places.

Why does the Favorites menu display items I did not add?

AOL automatically adds items to your list of favorite places. These items provide quick access to AOL areas you may find useful.

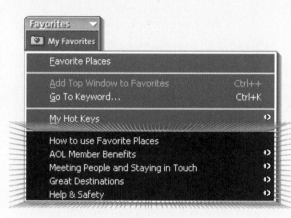

> **How to use Favorite Places**
> Provides information about using favorite places.

> **AOL Member Benefits**
> Provides information about services for AOL members.

> **Meeting People and Staying in Touch**
> Provides information about meeting people on AOL.

> **Great Destinations**
> Provides quick access to popular AOL areas.

> **Help & Safety**
> Provides access to help information and safety features.

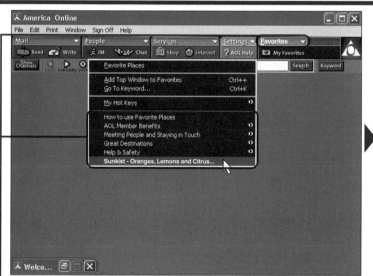

VIEW A FAVORITE PLACE

1 Click **Favorites**.

2 Click the favorite place you want to view.

Note: An item displaying an arrow (⊙) contains favorite places. To display the favorite places in an item displaying an arrow, position the mouse ⊠ over the item.

■ The favorite place you selected appears.

■ You can repeat steps **1** and **2** to view another favorite place.

You can create new folders to organize your list of favorite places.

For example, you can create a folder called Hobbies to keep all your hobby-related favorite places together.

ADD A FAVORITE PLACES FOLDER

1 Click **My Favorites**.

■ The Favorite Places window appears.

■ This area displays folders (📁) AOL automatically sets up and your favorite places (💜).

2 Click **Favorite Places** to create a main folder.

Note: To create a folder within another folder, click the folder (📁).

3 Click **New** to create a new folder.

Can I hide the contents of a favorite places folder?

Yes. Hiding the contents of a folder in the Favorite Places window can help reduce clutter in the window. To hide the contents of a folder, double-click the folder. You can double-click the folder again to display its contents.

Will my new folder appear on the Favorites menu?

Yes. When you add a new folder to the Favorite Places window, the folder also appears on the Favorites menu. Folders on the Favorites menu display an arrow (▶). To display the Favorites menu, see page 151.

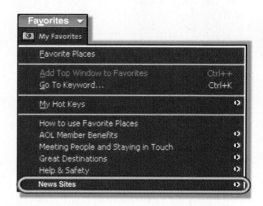

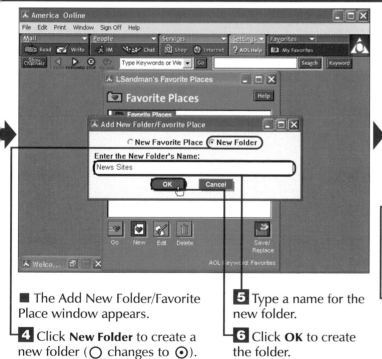

■ The Add New Folder/Favorite Place window appears.

4 Click **New Folder** to create a new folder (○ changes to ⊙).

5 Type a name for the new folder.

6 Click **OK** to create the folder.

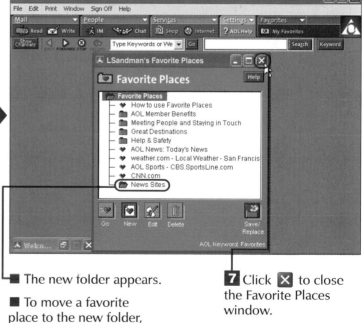

■ The new folder appears.

■ To move a favorite place to the new folder, see page 154.

7 Click ✕ to close the Favorite Places window.

MOVE A FAVORITE PLACE

You can move a favorite place to a new location in your list. For example, you may want to move a favorite place you frequently visit to the top of your list or move a favorite place to a folder.

You can move a folder the same way you move a favorite place.

MOVE A FAVORITE PLACE

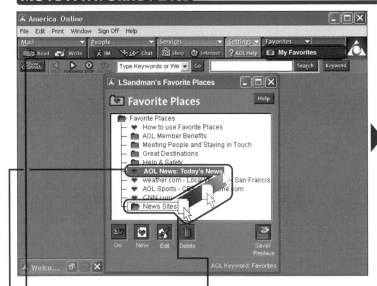

1 Click **My Favorites**.

■ The Favorite Places window appears.

2 Position the mouse ⬚ over the favorite place you want to move.

3 Drag the favorite place to a new location.

Note: The favorite place will appear above the favorite place (♥) that displays a border or in the folder (▦) that displays a border.

■ The favorite place appears in the new location.

DELETE A FAVORITE PLACE

You can delete a folder the same way you delete a favorite place. When you delete a folder, any favorite places stored in the folder will also be deleted.

DELETE A FAVORITE PLACE

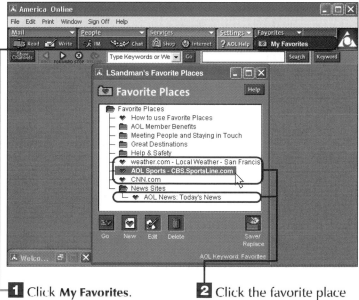

1 Click **My Favorites**.

■ The Favorite Places window appears.

2 Click the favorite place you want to delete.

3 Click **Delete** to delete the favorite place.

■ A confirmation dialog box appears.

4 Click **Yes** to delete the favorite place.

■ The favorite place disappears from the Favorite Places window.

ADD A FAVORITE PLACE TO A MESSAGE

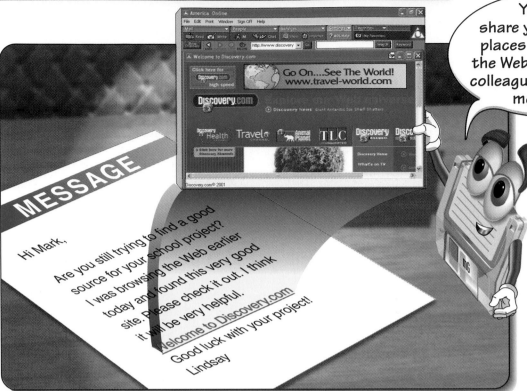

> You can share your favorite places on AOL and the Web with friends, colleagues and family members.

When you add a favorite place to a message, AOL inserts a link to the favorite place into the message. The person who receives the message can select the link to display the favorite place.

ADD A FAVORITE PLACE TO A MESSAGE

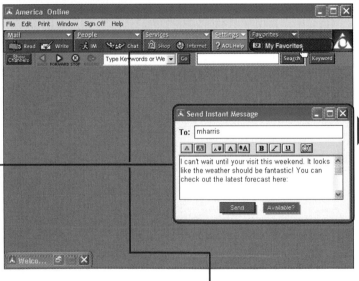

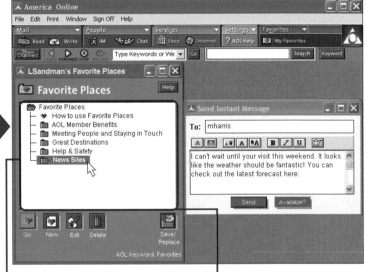

1 Compose the message you want to add a favorite place to.

Note: To compose an e-mail message, see page 44. To compose an instant message, see page 84.

2 Click **My Favorites** to add a favorite place to the message.

■ The Favorite Places window appears.

■ This area displays the organization of your favorite places.

■ A closed folder (📁) contains hidden favorite places.

3 To display the favorite places within a closed folder, double-click the folder (📁 changes to 📂).

156

Can I add favorite places to other types of messages?

Yes. You can perform the steps below to add a favorite place to a message you are sending to a message board. This allows you to share the favorite place with every member who reads the message board. To send a message to a message board, see page 126.

Will people who do not use AOL be able to display the favorite places I add to messages?

People who do not use AOL can display your favorite places on the Web, but only AOL members will be able to view your favorite places on AOL.

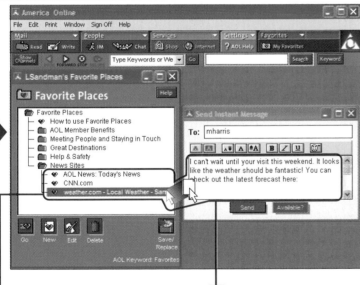

■ The favorite places within the folder appear.

4 Position the mouse over the favorite place you want to add to the message.

5 Drag the favorite place to the message.

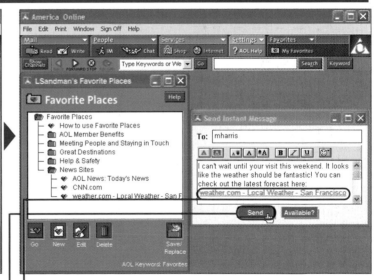

■ A link to the favorite place appears in the message. Links appear underlined and blue in color.

6 When you finish composing the message, click **Send** or **Send Now** to send the message.

Note: The name of the button depends on the type of message you are sending.

■ The person who receives the message will be able to click the link to display the favorite place.

CREATE A NEWS PROFILE

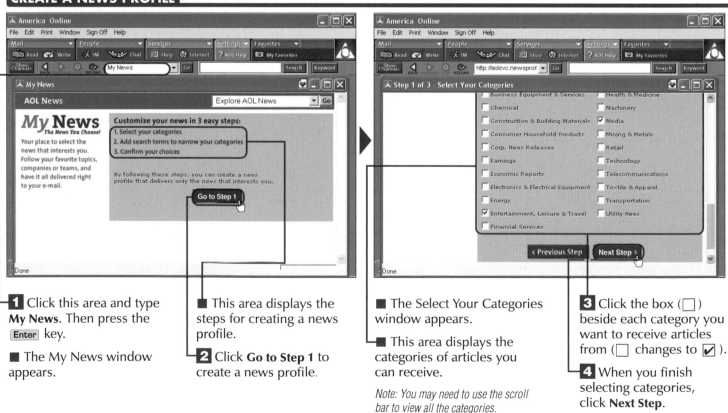

1 Click this area and type **My News**. Then press the Enter key.

■ The My News window appears.

■ This area displays the steps for creating a news profile.

2 Click **Go to Step 1** to create a news profile.

■ The Select Your Categories window appears.

■ This area displays the categories of articles you can receive.

Note: You may need to use the scroll bar to view all the categories.

3 Click the box (☐) beside each category you want to receive articles from (☐ changes to ☑).

4 When you finish selecting categories, click **Next Step**.

Can I create more than one news profile?

You can create up to five news profiles for each screen name set up on your AOL account. AOL will send each article to your online mailbox as one e-mail message. You should regularly check your mailbox for new messages since your mailbox can quickly fill up with messages.

How many categories should I select for a news profile?

You should select only one or two categories for a news profile. This will help ensure that the news profile delivers articles that are targeted to your specific interests. If you are interested in many categories, you can create separate news profiles for each category.

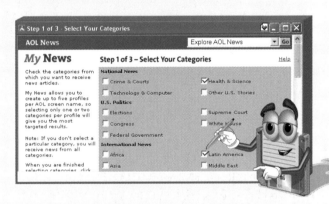

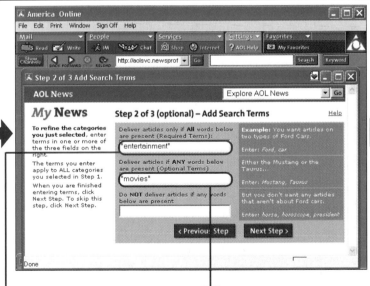

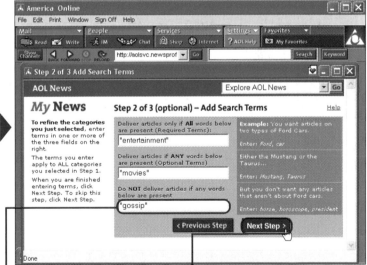

■ The Add Search Terms window appears.

5 To specify a word or phrase that must appear in each article you receive, click this area and type the word or phrase enclosed in quotation marks (").

6 To specify a word or phrase you want to appear in each article you receive, click this area and type the word or phrase enclosed in quotation marks (").

7 To specify a word or phrase you do not want to appear in each article you receive, click this area and type the word or phrase enclosed in quotation marks (").

Note: To enter more than one word or phrase in step 5, 6 or 7, separate each word or phrase with a comma (,).

8 Click **Next Step** to continue.

CONTINUED

When creating a news profile, you can specify the number of articles you want to receive each day.

25 articles per day

A news profile can deliver up to 200 articles a day to your online mailbox.

CREATE A NEWS PROFILE (CONTINUED)

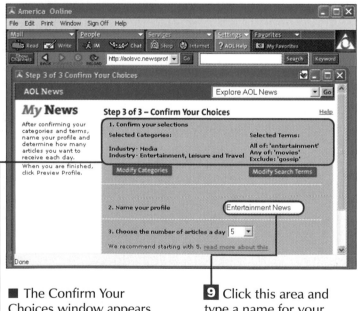

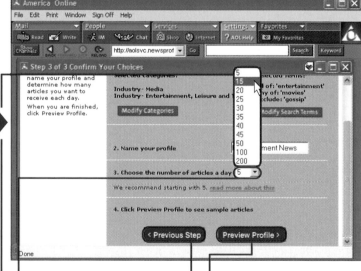

■ The Confirm Your Choices window appears.

■ This area displays the categories you selected and any search terms you specified.

9 Click this area and type a name for your news profile.

10 To choose the number of articles you want to receive each day, click this area. A menu appears.

11 Click the number of articles you want to receive each day.

12 Click **Preview Profile** to see samples of the types of articles you will receive.

Note: You may need to use the scroll bar to see the Preview Profile button.

■ You can click **Previous Step** to return to a previous step and change your selections.

How do I later create another news profile?

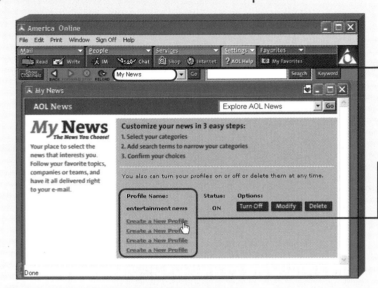

1 Click this area and type **My News**. Then press the Enter key.

■ The My News window appears.

■ This area displays the name of each news profile you have created.

2 Click **Create a New Profile**.

3 Perform steps **3** to **14** starting on page 158 to finish creating the news profile.

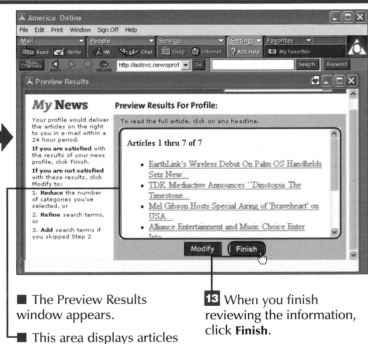

■ The Preview Results window appears.

■ This area displays articles that match the information you entered for your news profile. You can click an article to read the article.

13 When you finish reviewing the information, click **Finish**.

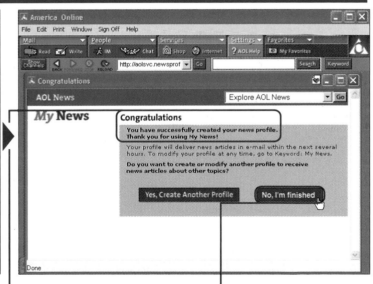

■ The Congratulations window appears.

■ This message appears when you have successfully set up your news profile. You will begin receiving articles within a few hours.

14 To finish creating news profiles, click **No, I'm finished**.

*Note: A dialog box may appear. Click **Yes** to close the dialog box.*

TURN OFF A NEWS PROFILE

You can temporarily turn off a news profile. This is useful when you go on vacation and do not want your online mailbox to fill up with messages.

TURN OFF A NEWS PROFILE

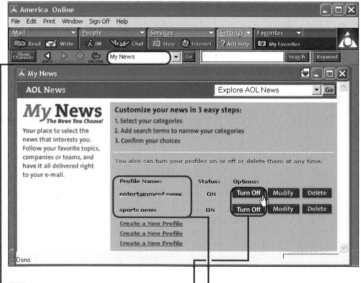

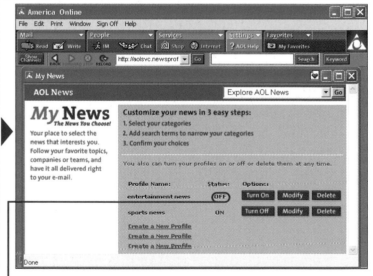

1 Click this area and type **My News**. Then press the Enter key.

■ The My News window appears.

■ This area displays the name of each news profile you have created.

2 Click **Turn Off** beside the news profile you want to turn off.

■ The status of the news profile changes from **On** to **Off**.

■ To once again receive articles for the news profile, repeat steps **1** and **2**, clicking **Turn On** in step **2**.

You can delete a news profile that delivers articles to your online mailbox that are no longer of interest to you.

DELETE A NEWS PROFILE

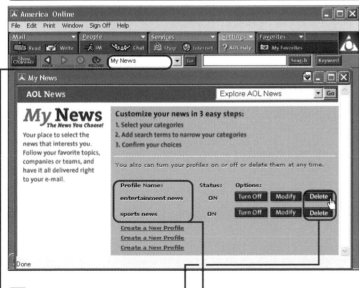

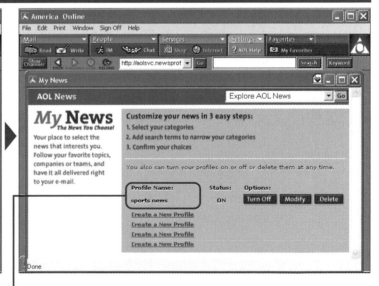

1 Click this area and type **My News**. Then press the Enter key.

■ The My News window appears.

■ This area displays the name of each news profile you have created.

2 Click **Delete** beside the news profile you want to delete.

■ The news profile disappears from the list of news profiles.

■ You will no longer receive articles from the news profile.

You can create a portfolio to track investments such as stocks and funds.

You can create up to 20 portfolios for each screen name set up on your AOL account. Each portfolio can contain different stocks and funds. For example, one portfolio can contain stocks you own and a second portfolio can contain stocks you want to monitor.

CREATE A STOCK PORTFOLIO

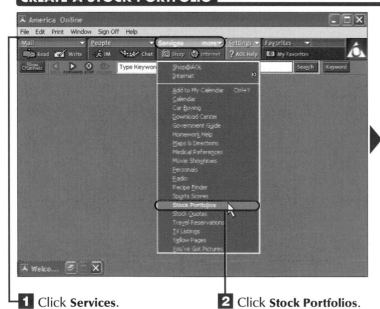

1 Click **Services**.

2 Click **Stock Portfolios**.

■ The My Portfolios window appears.

3 Click **Create** to create a new portfolio.

How can I find the symbol for a stock or fund I want to add to my portfolio?

You can use the Symbol Lookup link to find the symbol for a stock or fund.

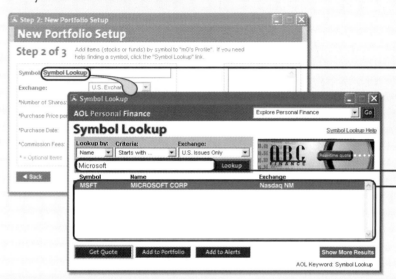

1 In the Step 2 window, click **Symbol Lookup**.

■ The Symbol Lookup window appears.

2 Type the company name of the stock or the name of the fund you want to find the symbol for. Then press the **Enter** key.

■ This area displays the symbol for the stock or fund.

Note: When you finish reviewing the information, click ✕ to close the Symbol Lookup window.

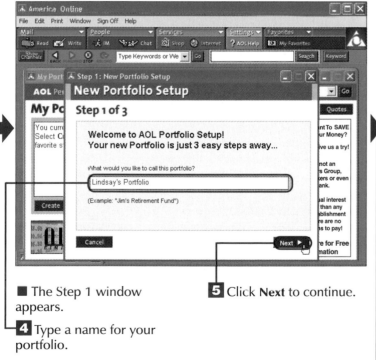

■ The Step 1 window appears.

4 Type a name for your portfolio.

5 Click **Next** to continue.

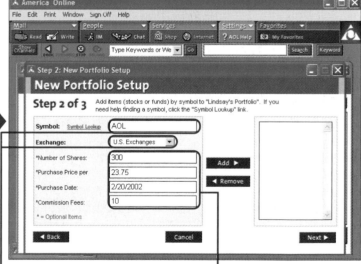

■ The Step 2 window appears.

6 Type the symbol for a stock or fund you want to add to your portfolio.

■ This area displays the exchange that offers the stock or fund. You can click this area to specify a different exchange.

7 Double-click each area and type the information for the stock or fund.

Note: You can leave the areas blank to monitor a stock or fund you do not own.

CONTINUED

165

CREATE A STOCK PORTFOLIO

You can add up to 100 different stocks and funds to each portfolio. AOL will keep track of each stock and fund.

When you add a stock or fund to a portfolio, you are not buying the stock or fund. Portfolios only allow you to keep track of your investments.

CREATE A STOCK PORTFOLIO (CONTINUED)

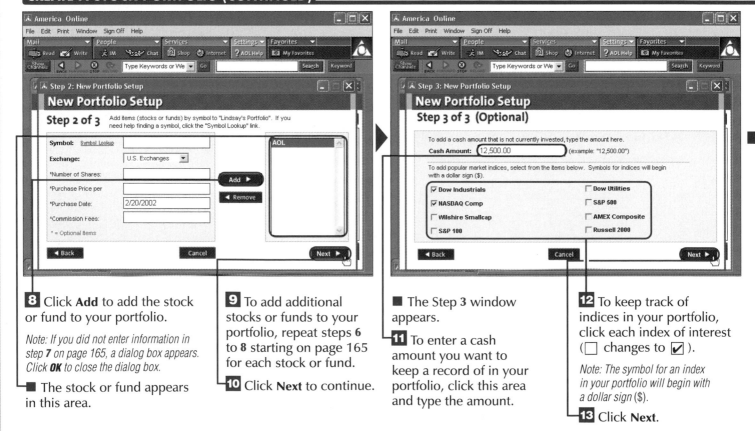

8 Click **Add** to add the stock or fund to your portfolio.

Note: If you did not enter information in step 7 on page 165, a dialog box appears. Click OK to close the dialog box.

■ The stock or fund appears in this area.

9 To add additional stocks or funds to your portfolio, repeat steps **6** to **8** starting on page 165 for each stock or fund.

10 Click **Next** to continue.

■ The Step **3** window appears.

11 To enter a cash amount you want to keep a record of in your portfolio, click this area and type the amount.

12 To keep track of indices in your portfolio, click each index of interest (☐ changes to ☑).

Note: The symbol for an index in your portfolio will begin with a dollar sign ($).

13 Click **Next**.

166

SIMPLIFY IT

How up to date is the information in my portfolio?

Unlike the newspaper, which reports the performance of stocks for the previous day, AOL updates the performance of stocks on a regular basis. For example, stock information is updated every 15 to 20 minutes and United States indices, such as the Dow Industrials, are always up to date.

SIMPLIFY IT

Where can I learn more about stocks and funds?

You can use the following keywords to display information that can help you learn more about stocks and funds. For information about using keywords, see page 24.

KEYWORDS

Business News	Online Investor
Investment Research	PF Community
Marketday	Quotes
MNC Stocks	Research a Company
Mutual Funds	Stock

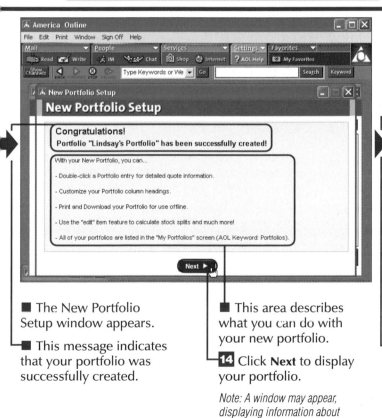

■ The New Portfolio Setup window appears.

■ This message indicates that your portfolio was successfully created.

■ This area describes what you can do with your new portfolio.

14 Click **Next** to display your portfolio.

*Note: A window may appear, displaying information about AOL's privacy policies. Click **OK** to close the window.*

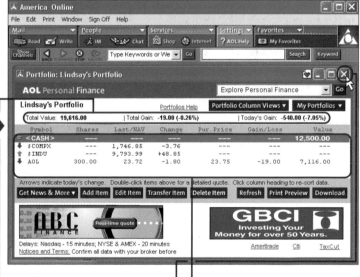

■ The Portfolio window appears.

■ This area displays the total value of the portfolio and the amount of change to the portfolio.

■ This area displays information about each item in the portfolio. An icon beside each item indicates if the item is up (⬆), down (⬇) or unchanged (⬅) in value.

15 When you finish viewing the portfolio, click ☒ to close the window.

DISPLAY A STOCK PORTFOLIO

You can display your portfolio at any time to check the performance of stocks and funds you are tracking.

Jim's Portfolio

Stock Report

NOW PLAYING

DISPLAY A STOCK PORTFOLIO

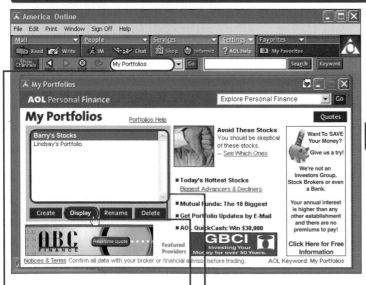

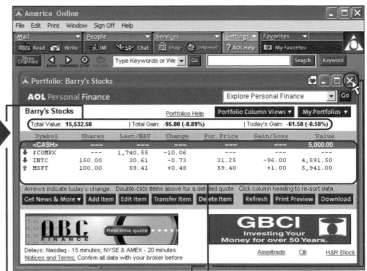

1 Click this area and type **My Portfolios**. Then press the Enter key.

■ The My Portfolios window appears.

■ This area displays the name of each portfolio you have created.

2 Click the name of the portfolio you want to display.

3 Click **Display** to display the portfolio.

■ The Portfolio window appears.

■ This area displays the total value of the portfolio and the amount of change to the portfolio.

■ This area displays information about each item in the portfolio. An icon beside each item indicates if the item is up (↑), down (↓) or unchanged (=) in value.

4 When you finish viewing the portfolio, click ✕ to close the Portfolio window.

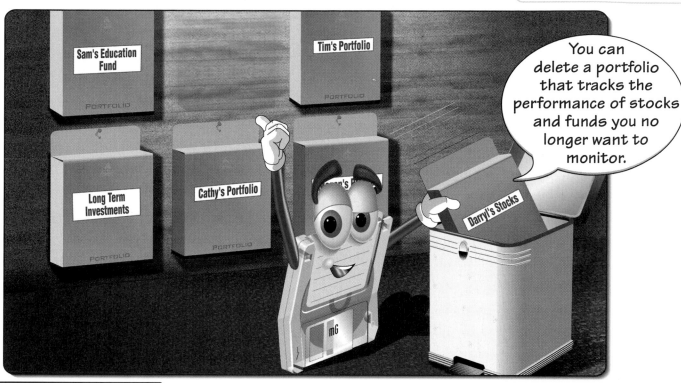

DELETE A STOCK PORTFOLIO

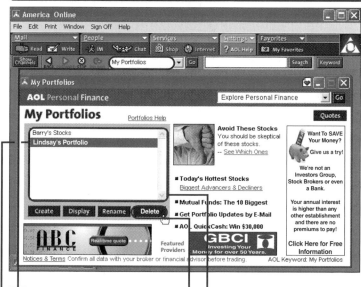

1 Click this area and type **My Portfolios**. Then press the Enter key.

■ The My Portfolios window appears.

■ This area displays the name of each portfolio you have created.

2 Click the name of the portfolio you want to delete.

3 Click **Delete** to delete the portfolio.

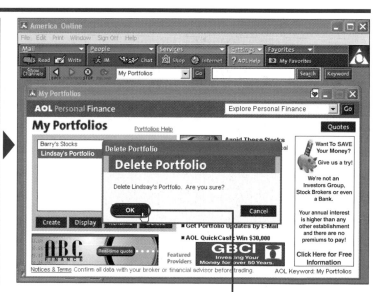

■ A confirmation dialog box appears.

4 Click **OK** to delete the portfolio.

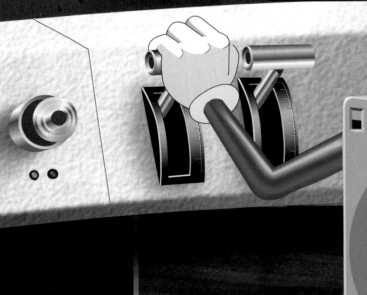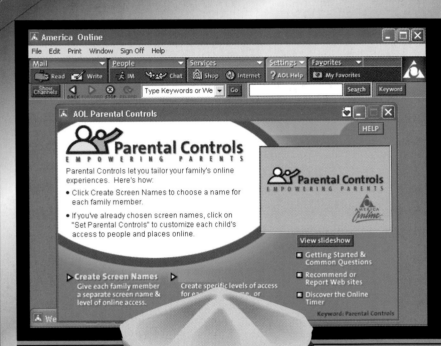

WORK WITH PASSWORDS AND SCREEN NAMES

Do you want to learn how to change your password or create a new screen name? This chapter will teach you how.

CHANGE YOUR PASSWORD

You should regularly change your password to prevent others from accessing your AOL account.

A person who knows your password will have full access to your AOL account.

CHANGE YOUR PASSWORD

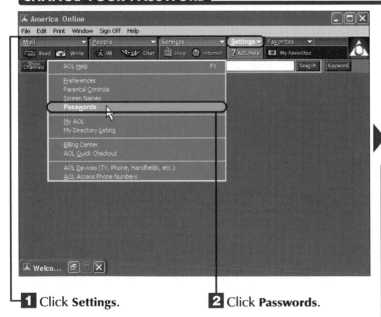

1 Click **Settings**.

2 Click **Passwords**.

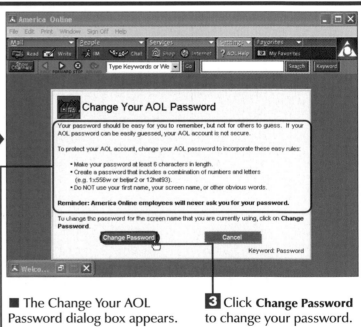

■ The Change Your AOL Password dialog box appears.

■ This area displays information about changing your password.

3 Click **Change Password** to change your password.

■ The Change Your Password dialog box appears.

What password should I use?

You should follow these guidelines when choosing a password.

➤ A password should be easy for you to remember, but difficult for others to guess.

➤ Do not use your first name, screen name or other obvious words for your password.

➤ A password must be at least six characters long.

➤ A password should contain both letters and numbers, such as happy12.

While online, what should I do if an AOL staff member asks for my password?

An AOL staff member will never ask for your password or credit card information online. To keep your AOL account secure, you should never give your password to anyone. If you are concerned that someone may know your password, you should change the password immediately.

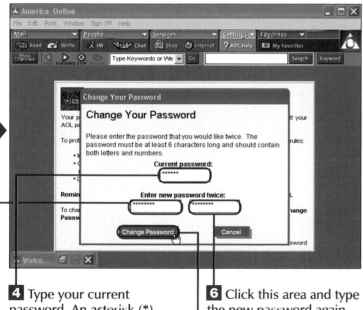

4 Type your current password. An asterisk (*) appears for each character you type to prevent others from seeing your password.

5 Click this area and type a new password.

6 Click this area and type the new password again.

7 Click **Change Password**.

■ A confirmation dialog box appears, stating that your password has been changed.

8 Click **OK** to close the dialog box.

9 Click **Cancel** to close the Change Your AOL Password dialog box.

■ If you stored your password so you do not have to type the password each time you connect to AOL, you must update your stored password. To store the new password, see page 174.

You can store your password so you do not have to type the password each time you connect to AOL.

If you store your password, anyone with access to your computer will be able to use your account to connect to AOL.

You may have chosen to store your password when you first connected to AOL.

STORE YOUR PASSWORD

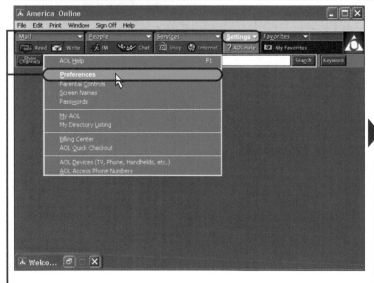

1 Click **Settings**.

2 Click **Preferences**.

■ The Preferences window appears.

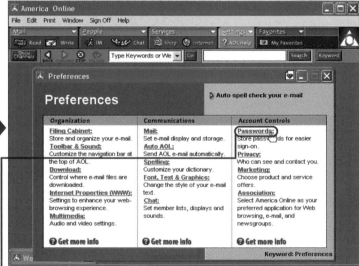

3 Click **Passwords** to store your password.

■ The Password Preferences window appears.

Can I stop storing my password?

You can stop storing your password at any time. Perform steps **1** to **3** below to display the Password Preferences window. Then perform steps **5** and **6** to stop storing your password (☑ changes to ☐ in step **5**).

How can I store the password for another screen name set up on my AOL account?

To store the password for another screen name, you must first connect to AOL using the screen name you want to store the password for. You can then perform the steps below to store the password for the screen name. You should use a different password for each screen name set up on your AOL account. For information about creating a screen name, see page 176.

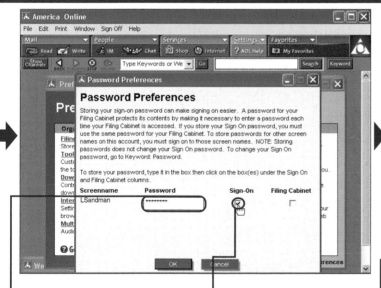

4 Click this area and type your password. An asterisk (*) appears for each character you type to prevent others from seeing your password.

Note: If asterisks already appear in the area, drag the mouse ⌶ over the asterisks and then type your password.

5 Click this option to store your password (☐ changes to ☑).

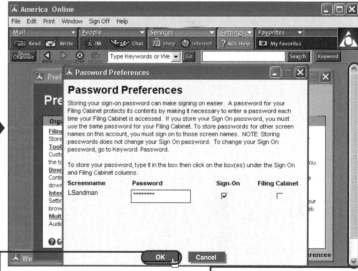

6 Click **OK** to save your changes.

■ You may need to use the scroll bar to view the OK button.

You can create a screen name to allow a family member or friend to use your AOL account.

An AOL account can have up to seven screen names.

A screen name identifies each person on AOL. You cannot use the same screen name as another AOL member.

CREATE A SCREEN NAME

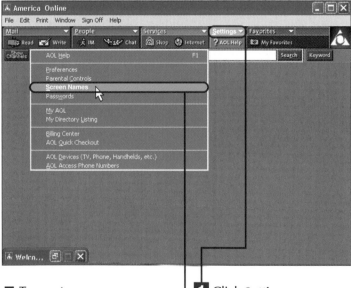

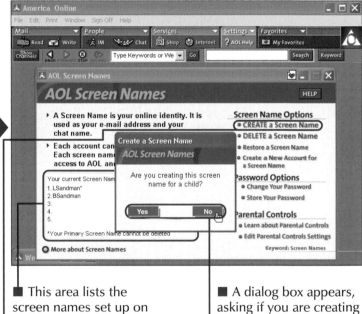

■ To create a screen name, you must connect to AOL using the primary screen name. The primary screen name is the name you chose when you first set up your AOL account. To connect to AOL, see page 6.

1 Click **Settings**.

2 Click **Screen Names**.

■ The AOL Screen Names window appears.

■ This area lists the screen names set up on your AOL account. The primary screen name displays an asterisk (*).

3 Click **Create a Screen Name**.

■ A dialog box appears, asking if you are creating the screen name for a child.

4 Click **Yes** or **No** to specify whether the screen name is for a child.

What screen name should I use?

Your screen name is your e-mail address and identifies you in AOL areas such as chat rooms and message boards. You should follow these guidelines when choosing a screen name.

➤ A screen name can be your real name or a nickname.

➤ Do not use a child's full name as a screen name.

➤ A screen name can contain letters, numbers and spaces.

➤ A screen name must start with a letter.

➤ A screen name can be 3 to 16 characters long.

```
s u p e r   j o h n n y   3 3 3
1 2 3 4 5 6 7 8 9 10 11 12 13 14 15 16
```

Will AOL keep the information for my screen name separate from other screen names I create?

AOL keeps the information for each screen name on your account separate. For example, each screen name you create will have its own password, e-mail address, Buddy List, filing cabinet and preferences.

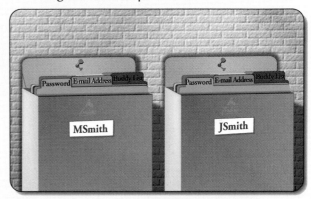

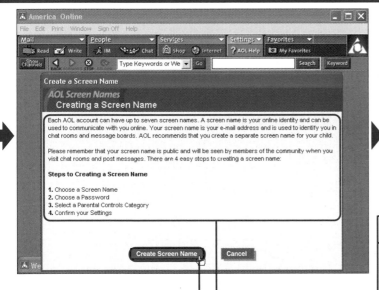

■ The Create a Screen Name dialog box appears.

*Note: If you selected **Yes** in step 4, the Important Note to Parents dialog box appears, displaying information for parents. Click **Continue** to close the dialog box.*

■ This area displays information about creating a screen name.

5 Click **Create Screen Name**.

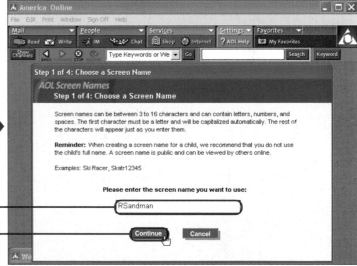

■ The Choose a Screen Name dialog box appears.

6 Type the screen name you want to use.

7 Click **Continue**.

*Note: A message will appear if you typed a screen name that another member has already chosen. Click **OK** to close the message and try another screen name.*

CONTINUED

When creating a screen name, you must select the appropriate age group for the person who will use the screen name.

Choosing an age group helps parents control the information their children can access.

CREATE A SCREEN NAME (CONTINUED)

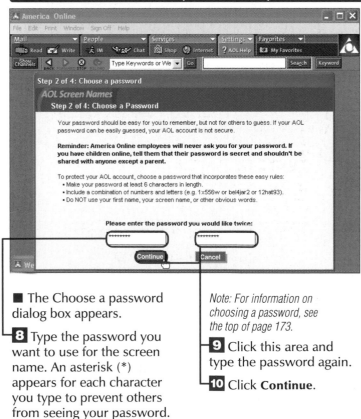

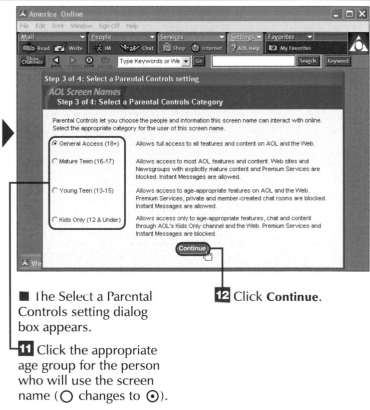

■ The Choose a password dialog box appears.

8 Type the password you want to use for the screen name. An asterisk (*) appears for each character you type to prevent others from seeing your password.

Note: For information on choosing a password, see the top of page 173.

9 Click this area and type the password again.

10 Click **Continue**.

■ The Select a Parental Controls setting dialog box appears.

11 Click the appropriate age group for the person who will use the screen name (○ changes to ⊙).

12 Click **Continue**.

Can I later change the age group I selected for a screen name?

You can change the parental controls to change the age group for a screen name you created. Changing the age group for a screen name is useful when a child is ready for a new age group. To change parental controls, see page 184.

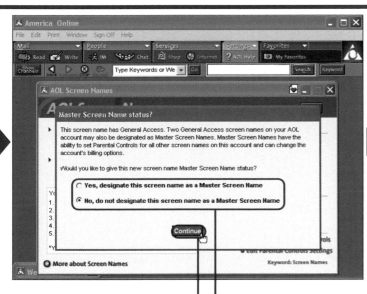

Should I make the screen name I am creating a master screen name?

If the screen name is for an adult you trust to perform tasks that will affect your AOL account, you can make the screen name a master screen name. A person with a master screen name will be able to perform the same tasks you can perform with your primary screen name. For example, the person will be able to create and delete screen names, change the parental controls for screen names and change the billing information for your AOL account.

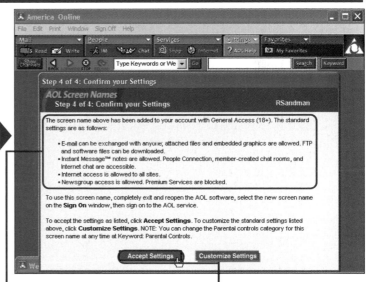

■ The Master Screen Name status dialog box appears if you selected **General Access** in step **11**.

*Note: If the dialog box does not appear, skip to step **15**.*

13 Click the circle (○) beside an option to specify if you want the screen name to be a master screen name (○ changes to ⊙).

Note: For information about master screen names, see the top of this page.

14 Click **Continue**.

■ The Confirm your Settings dialog box appears.

■ This area displays information about the screen name, such as the type of access given to the screen name.

15 Click **Accept Settings**.

■ To use the new screen name, exit and reconnect to AOL. To connect to AOL, see page 6.

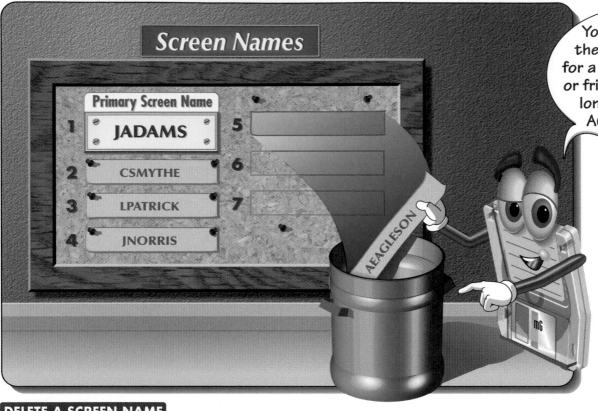

> You can delete the screen name for a family member or friend who will no longer use your AOL account.

You cannot delete the primary screen name. The primary screen name is the name you chose when you first set up your AOL account.

DELETE A SCREEN NAME

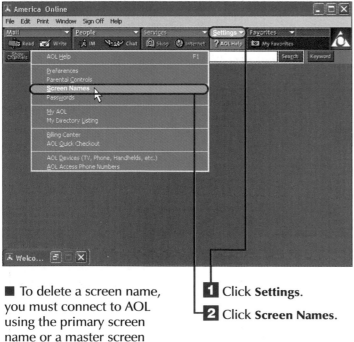

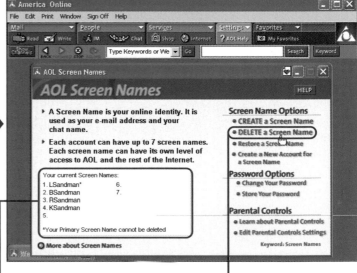

■ To delete a screen name, you must connect to AOL using the primary screen name or a master screen name. To connect to AOL, see page 6.

1 Click **Settings**.

2 Click **Screen Names**.

■ The AOL Screen Names window appears.

■ This area lists the screen names set up on your AOL account. The primary screen name displays an asterisk (*).

3 Click **Delete a Screen Name**.

Can I restore a screen name I accidentally deleted?

You may be able to restore a screen name up to six months after you delete the screen name.

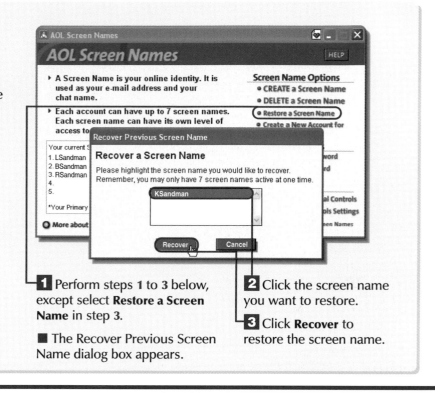

1 Perform steps **1** to **3** below, except select **Restore a Screen Name** in step **3**.

■ The Recover Previous Screen Name dialog box appears.

2 Click the screen name you want to restore.

3 Click **Recover** to restore the screen name.

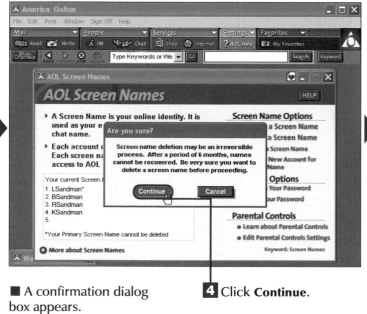

■ A confirmation dialog box appears.

4 Click **Continue**.

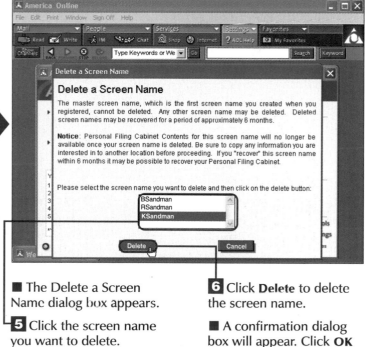

■ The Delete a Screen Name dialog box appears.

5 Click the screen name you want to delete.

6 Click **Delete** to delete the screen name.

■ A confirmation dialog box will appear. Click **OK** to close the dialog box.

When you finish using AOL, a family member or friend can switch to their screen name without having to exit and then reconnect to AOL.

Switching screen names allows a family member or friend to check for new messages and use AOL with their own preferences. To create screen names, see page 176.

SWITCH SCREEN NAMES

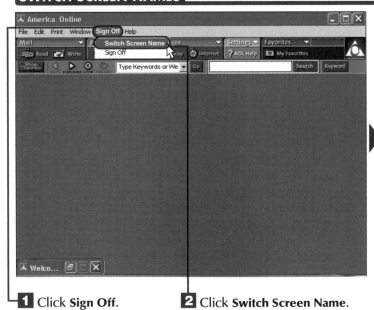

1 Click **Sign Off**.

2 Click **Switch Screen Name**.

■ The Switch Screen Names window appears.

■ This area lists the screen names set up on your AOL account, the number of new e-mail messages for each screen name and the parental controls setting for each screen name.

Note: For information about parental controls, see page 184.

3 Click the screen name you want to switch to.

4 Click **Switch**.

Can I work in the America Online window without being connected to AOL?

Yes. You can sign off AOL to work in the America Online window without being connected to AOL. This is useful when you want to keep your telephone line free while performing tasks such as creating e-mail messages.

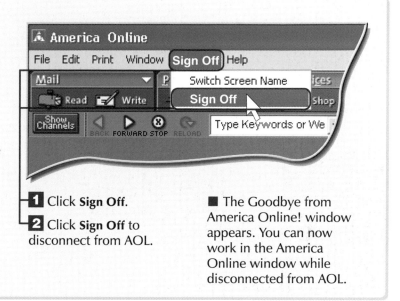

■1 Click **Sign Off**.

■2 Click **Sign Off** to disconnect from AOL.

■ The Goodbye from America Online! window appears. You can now work in the America Online window while disconnected from AOL.

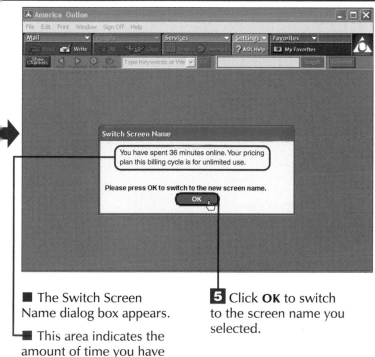

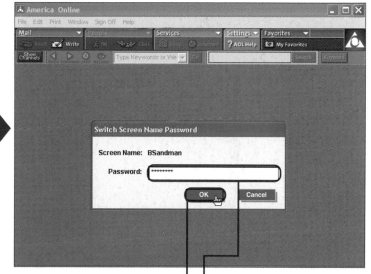

■ The Switch Screen Name dialog box appears.

■ This area indicates the amount of time you have spent online.

■5 Click **OK** to switch to the screen name you selected.

■ The Switch Screen Name Password dialog box appears.

Note: This dialog box will not appear if you stored the password for the screen name. To store a password, see page 174.

■6 Type the password for the screen name. An asterisk (*) appears for each character you type to prevent others from seeing the password.

■7 Click **OK** to connect to AOL using the new screen name.

You can control the type of information your children can access on AOL and the Internet.

You first set up the parental controls for a child when you created a screen name for the child. As the child matures, you may want to change the type of access given to the child. For information about creating a screen name, see page 176.

CHANGE PARENTAL CONTROLS

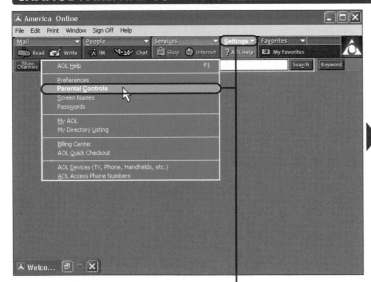

■ To change parental controls, you must connect to AOL using the primary screen name or a master screen name. The primary screen name is the name you chose when you first set up your AOL account. To connect to AOL, see page 6.

1 Click **Settings**.

2 Click **Parental Controls**.

■ The AOL Parental Controls window appears.

3 Click **Set Parental Controls** to change the parental controls for screen names set up on your account.

What types of information can I restrict using parental controls?

Web
Restrict access to sites on the Web.

Instant Messages
Restrict the ability to exchange instant messages with other AOL members.

E-mail
Restrict features for exchanging e-mail messages with people on AOL and the Internet.

Chat
Restrict access to chat rooms, which allow AOL members to have online conversations.

Download Files
Restrict the ability to transfer files to your computer.

Premium Services
Restrict access to services that charge a fee to your AOL account.

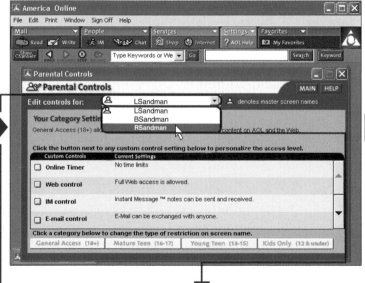

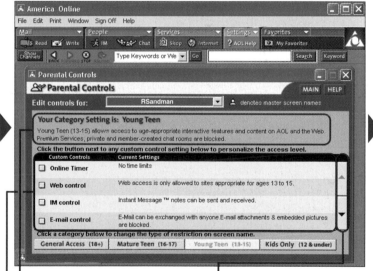 

■ The Parental Controls window appears.

4 Click this area to display a list of the screen names set up on your account.

5 Click the screen name you want to change the parental controls for.

■ This area displays the category the screen name belongs to and a brief description of the category.

■ This area displays information about the type of access the screen name has on AOL and the Internet.

■ You can click ⊡ or ⊡ to browse through the information.

CONTINUED

CHANGE PARENTAL CONTROLS

You can choose from four different categories to determine the type of information your child can access. Each category has a different level of access to AOL and the Internet.

Kids Only
○ 12 and under

Young Teen
○ 13 to 15

Mature Teen
○ 16 to 17

General Access
● 18 and older

CHANGE PARENTAL CONTROLS (CONTINUED)

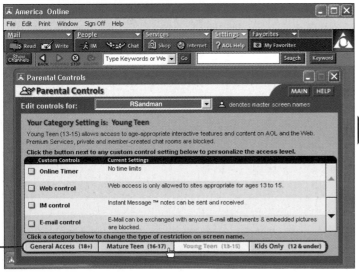

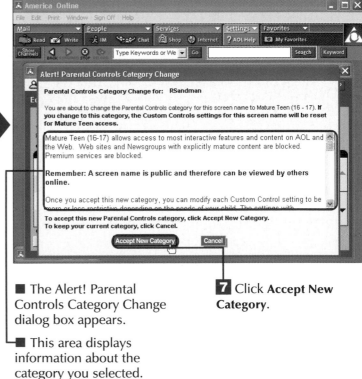

6 Click the category for the type of access you want to set for the screen name.

Note: If all the categories are dimmed, the screen name has master screen name status and the category cannot be changed.

■ The Alert! Parental Controls Category Change dialog box appears.

■ This area displays information about the category you selected.

7 Click **Accept New Category.**

How can I further protect my children?

In addition to using AOL's parental controls, you should supervise your children when they are online. You can help keep your children safe by making sure they follow these guidelines.

➤ Do not give your full name, AOL password, home address, school name or telephone number to anyone you meet online.

➤ Do not agree to meet anyone in person.

➤ If someone makes you feel unsafe or uncomfortable, tell a parent immediately.

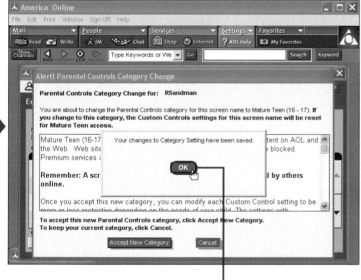

■ A confirmation dialog box appears.

8 Click **OK** to close the dialog box.

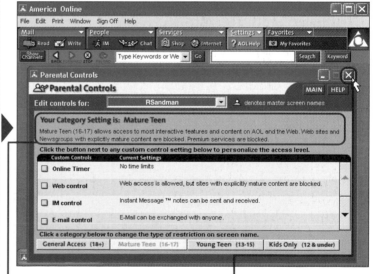

■ This area displays information about the category you selected for the screen name.

■ To change the parental controls for other screen names, repeat steps **4** to **8** starting on page 185 for each screen name.

9 When you finish changing parental controls, click ☒ to close the Parental Controls window.

CHAPTER 13

COOL AOL FEATURES

Would you like to play a music CD while you work on AOL? Are you interested in downloading files from AOL? Read this chapter to learn about the cool features AOL offers.

You can subscribe to one of AOL's free newsletters to have information about a topic that interests you delivered to your online mailbox.

AOL will deliver most newsletters to your online mailbox once a week.

AOL offers a variety of newsletters organized into categories such as Computers & Internet, Health and Travel.

SUBSCRIBE TO A NEWSLETTER

1 Click this area and type **Newsletter**. Then press the Enter key.

■ The Newsletter Center window appears.

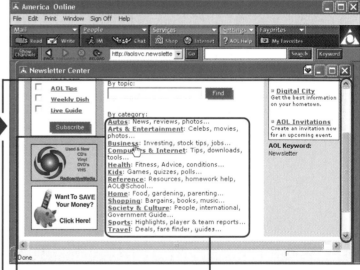

■ This area displays the categories of newsletters offered by AOL.

■ You may need to use the scroll bar to view all the categories.

2 Click a category of interest to display the newsletters in the category.

How can I view a list of the newsletters I am subscribed to?

In the Newsletter Center window, click the **View my current Newsletters** link to display a list of the newsletters you are subscribed to.

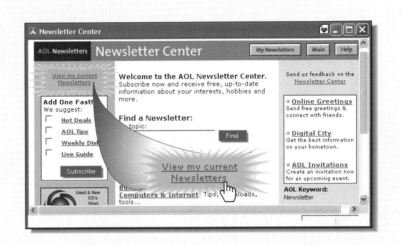

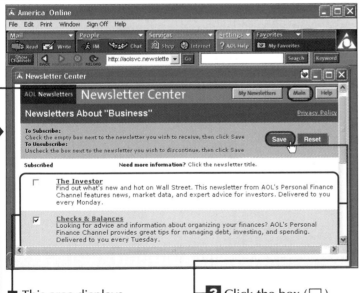

■ This area displays the name and a short description of each newsletter in the category you selected.

■ To return to the list of categories so you can view the newsletters in another category, click **Main**.

3 Click the box (☐) beside a newsletter you want to subscribe to (☐ changes to ☑).

■ You can repeat step 3 for each newsletter you want to subscribe to in the category.

4 Click **Save** to subscribe to the newsletter.

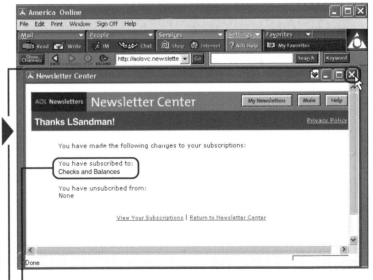

■ This area displays the name of the newsletter you subscribed to.

5 Click ☒ to close the Newsletter Center window.

■ To unsubscribe from a newsletter, repeat steps 1 to 5, clicking the box beside the newsletter you want to unsubscribe from in step 3 (☑ changes to ☐).

USING RADIO@AOL

You can use Radio@AOL to listen to music stations on AOL.

Radio@AOL offers a wide variety of stations organized into categories such as Classic Rock & Oldies, Jazz & Blues and Pop.

You need a computer with a sound card and speakers to listen to stations on Radio@AOL.

USING RADIO@AOL

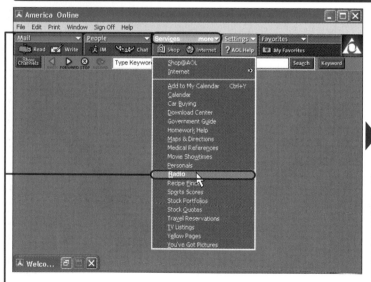

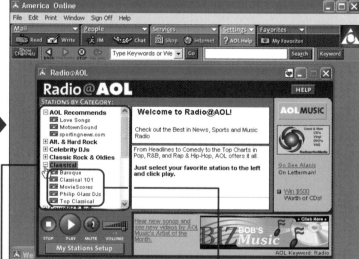

1 Click **Services**.

2 Click **Radio**.

■ The Radio@AOL window appears.

*Note: A dialog box may appear, describing Radio@AOL. Click **Enjoy Radio@AOL Now!** to close the dialog box.*

3 This area displays a list of station categories. To view the stations in a category, click the plus sign (⊞) beside the category (⊞ changes to ⊟).

■ A list of stations in the category appears. Stations display the 📻 symbol.

Note: To once again hide the stations in a category, click the minus sign (⊟) beside the category (⊟ changes to ⊞).

Can I have Radio@AOL remember my favorite stations?

Yes. You can store your favorite stations in the My Stations category. AOL creates the My Stations category the first time you add a station to the category.

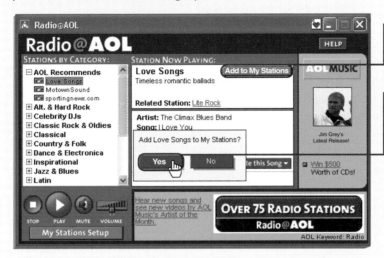

1 To add the station you are currently playing to the My Stations category, click **Add to My Stations**.

2 A confirmation dialog box appears. Click **Yes** to add the station to the My Stations category.

■ AOL stores the station in the My Stations category. You can play the stations in the My Stations category as you would play the stations in any category.

4 Click the station you want to play.

5 Click ▶ to play the station.

■ After a moment, the station begins to play.

■ This area displays the name of the station and a description of the station.

■ This area displays information about the current song, such as the name of the song and how much longer the song will play.

6 To decrease or increase the volume of the station, drag this slider (■) left or right.

7 To temporarily turn off the sound, click ◉.

Note: To once again turn on the sound, repeat step 7.

8 To stop playing the station at any time, click ◉.

9 When you finish listening to stations, click ✕ to close the Radio@AOL window.

PLAY A MUSIC CD

You can use AOL Media Player to play music CDs while you work with AOL.

You need a computer with a sound card, speakers and a CD-ROM drive to play music CDs.

PLAY A MUSIC CD

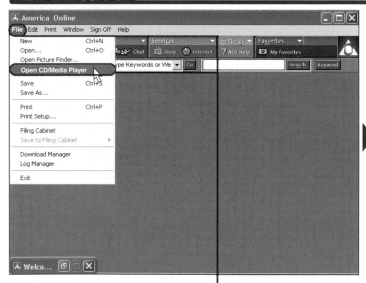

1 Insert a music CD into your CD-ROM drive.

*Note: If a dialog box appears, click **Cancel** to close the dialog box.*

2 Click **File**.

3 Click **Open CD/Media Player**.

■ The AOL Media Player window appears and the first song on the CD begins to play.

■ This area displays the name of the song that is currently playing.

■ This slider (▯) indicates the progress of the current song.

■ This area displays the amount of time the current song has been playing.

I adjusted the volume, but the music is still too loud. What can I do?

Your computer's speakers may have volume controls. If the volume is still too loud or too soft after you adjust the volume using AOL Media Player, you can use the volume controls on your speakers to change the volume.

Can I listen to a music CD privately?

You can listen to a music CD privately by plugging headphones into the jack at the front of your CD-ROM drive or into your speakers. If your CD-ROM drive or speakers do not have a headphone jack, you can plug the headphones into the back of your computer where you normally plug in the speakers.

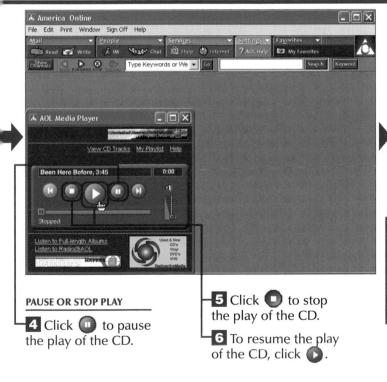

PAUSE OR STOP PLAY

4 Click ⏸ to pause the play of the CD.

5 Click ⏹ to stop the play of the CD.

6 To resume the play of the CD, click ▶.

ADJUST THE VOLUME

7 To increase or decrease the volume, drag this slider (▣) up or down.

PLAY ANOTHER SONG

8 Click one of the following options to play another song on the CD.

⏮ Play the previous song

⏭ Play the next song

CONTINUED

PLAY A MUSIC CD

> When playing a music CD, you can display a list of all the songs on the CD. You can select a song from the list to quickly play the song.

PLAY A MUSIC CD (CONTINUED)

VIEW A LIST OF SONGS

9 Click **View CD Tracks** to display a list of the songs on the CD.

■ The AOL CD Player Tracks window appears.

■ This area displays a list of the songs on the CD. You can use the scroll bar to browse through the list.

10 To play a specific song on the CD, click the name of the song.

11 Click **Play Track.**

How does AOL Media Player know the name of each song on my music CD?

When you play a music CD, AOL Media Player obtains information about the CD from the Internet and stores the information on your computer. Each time you play the CD, AOL will recognize the CD and display the appropriate information. If information about the CD you are playing is unavailable, AOL Media Player displays the track number of each song instead.

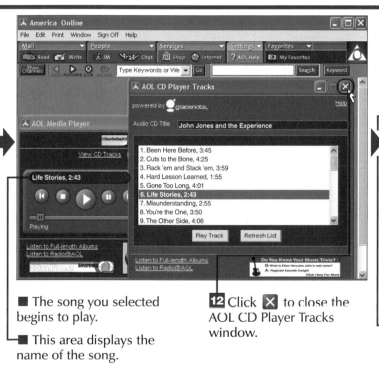

■ The song you selected begins to play.

■ This area displays the name of the song.

12 Click ✕ to close the AOL CD Player Tracks window.

CLOSE AOL MEDIA PLAYER

13 When you finish listening to the CD, click ✕ to close the AOL Media Player window.

14 Remove the CD from your CD-ROM drive.

FIND FILES TO DOWNLOAD

When you transfer information to your computer, you are "downloading" the information.

AOL organizes files into groups such as Fun & Games, Graphics, Internet Tools and Music & Sound.

FIND FILES TO DOWNLOAD—BY BROWSING

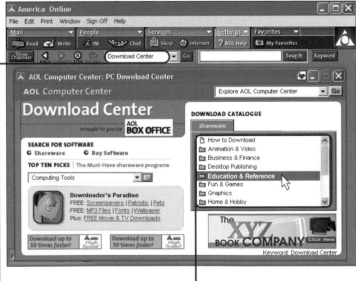

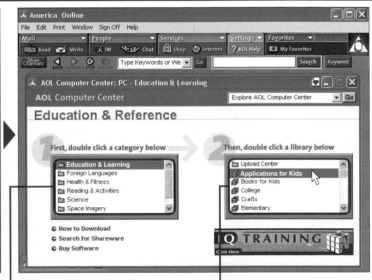

1 Click this area and type **Download Center**. Then press the Enter key.

■ The AOL Computer Center: PC Download Center window appears.

■ This area displays the groups of files available on AOL.

2 Double-click a group of interest.

■ A window for the group you selected appears.

■ This area lists the categories in the group.

3 Double-click a category of interest.

■ This area lists the file collections in the category you selected.

4 Double-click a file collection of interest.

What is the difference between freeware, shareware and demoware files?

Freeware

Freeware files are available to everyone free of charge. Freeware files are also labeled "freely distributed," "public domain" and "public distribution."

Shareware

Shareware files are programs that you can use free of charge for a limited period of time. If you want to continue using the program, you must purchase the program.

Demoware

Demoware or "demos" are sample versions of commercial programs that usually work only for a short period of time or have other limitations. For example, you may be able to play only a few levels in a game.

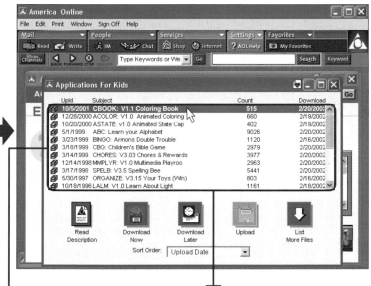

■ A window for the file collection you selected appears.

■ This area lists the available files.

5 To view a description of a file, double-click the file.

■ A window appears, displaying information about the file, including the file name, estimated transfer time and any equipment and software needed to use the file.

■ You can also determine if the file is freeware, shareware or demoware.

6 When you finish viewing the information, click ☒ to close the window.

■ To download a file, see page 202.

CONTINUED

FIND FILES TO DOWNLOAD

You can search through thousands of files offered on AOL to find files you want to download.

FIND FILES TO DOWNLOAD—BY SEARCHING

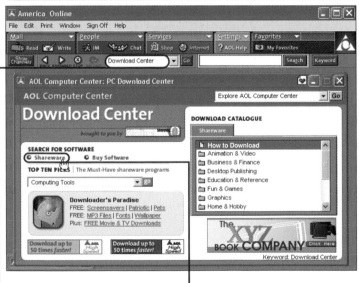

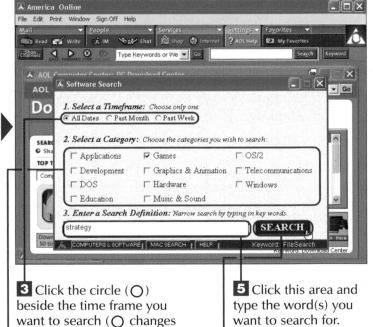

1 Click this area and type **Download Center**. Then press the Enter key.

■ The AOL Computer Center: PC Download Center window appears.

2 Click **Shareware** to search for files you can download.

■ The Software Search window appears.

3 Click the circle (○) beside the time frame you want to search (○ changes to ⊙).

4 Click the box (☐) beside each category you want to search (☐ changes to ☑).

5 Click this area and type the word(s) you want to search for.

6 Click **Search** to start the search.

What types of files can I download?

You can download several types of files to your computer, including image, sound, text, video and program files. Every file has a name and an extension, separated by a period (.). The name describes the contents of a file. The extension identifies the type of file. Here are some common file extensions.

File Extension	Type of File
.gif, .jpeg, .bmp	Image
.midi, .wav	Sound
.txt, .doc	Text
.avi	Video
.exe	Program
.zip	Compressed

Note: Many large files are compressed, or squeezed, to make them smaller. Compressed files require less storage space and transfer more quickly. Before you can use a compressed file, the file must be decompressed. The AOL software will automatically decompress files you download.

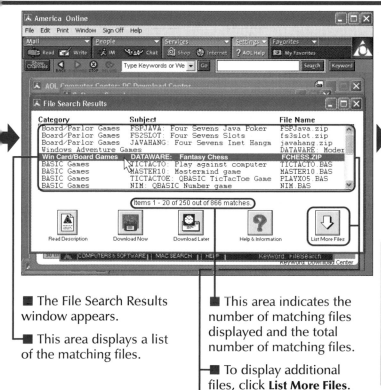

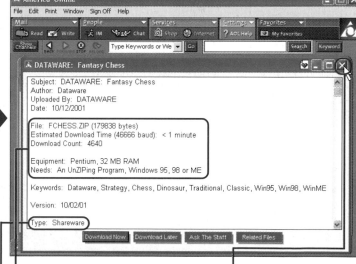

■ The File Search Results window appears.

■ This area displays a list of the matching files.

■ This area indicates the number of matching files displayed and the total number of matching files.

■ To display additional files, click **List More Files**.

7 To view a description of a file, double-click the file.

■ A window appears, displaying information about the file, including the file name, estimated transfer time and any equipment and software needed to use the file.

■ You can also determine if the software is freeware, shareware or demoware. For more information, see the top of page 199.

8 When you finish viewing the information, click ☒ to close the window.

■ To download a file, see page 202.

When you find a file of interest on AOL, you can download the file so you can use the file on your computer.

You must have the necessary hardware and software installed on your computer to display or play the file you download. For example, you will need a sound card and speakers to hear sound files.

DOWNLOAD A FILE

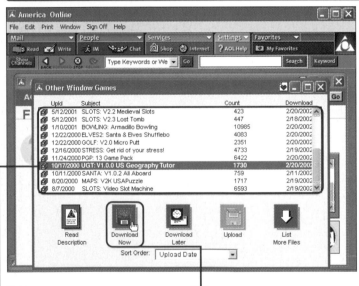

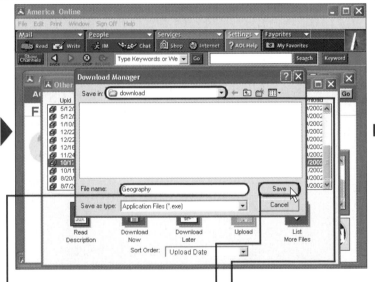

1 Click the file you want to download.

Note: To find a file you want to download, see pages 198 to 201.

2 Click **Download Now** to transfer the file to your computer.

■ The Download Manager dialog box appears.

3 This area displays the name of the file. To use a different name, type a new name.

■ This area shows the location where the file will be stored. You can click this area to change the location.

4 Click **Save** to start transferring the file to your computer.

How long will it take for a file to transfer to my computer?

The size of the file and the speed of your connection determine how long the file will take to transfer. You can reduce the time a file takes to transfer by downloading the file when fewer members are using AOL. Most members use AOL on evenings and weekends. Excessive noise on your telephone line can also increase the time a file takes to transfer. You can try signing off and signing on again to get a better connection.

Do I need to check files I download for viruses?

Although AOL checks many files for viruses before making the files available, you should also use an anti-virus program, such as McAfee's VirusScan, to check files you download for viruses. A virus is a program that can damage the information stored on your computer. You can use the keyword **virus** to learn more about viruses and get the latest anti-virus software. For information about using keywords, see page 24.

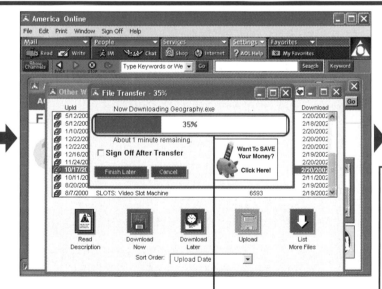

■ The File Transfer window appears.

■ This area indicates the progress of the transfer.

■ When the transfer is complete, a dialog box may appear, asking if you want to locate the file on your computer.

5 Click **No** to locate the file later. To locate files you have downloaded, see page 204.

■ To locate the file now, click **Yes**. A window will appear, displaying the contents of the folder that contains the file.

Note: The contents of some files will automatically appear on your screen.

You can use the Download Manager to locate files on your computer that you have downloaded.

You will find most downloaded files in the download folder, located inside the America Online 7.0 folder on your hard drive (C:).

LOCATE FILES YOU HAVE DOWNLOADED

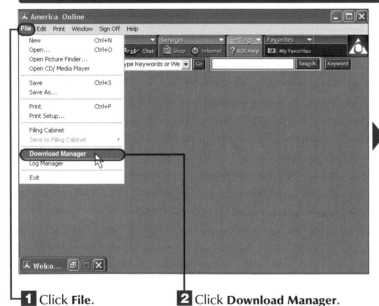

1 Click **File**.

2 Click **Download Manager**.

■ The Download Manager window appears.

3 Click **Show Files Downloaded**.

How can I view a description of a file I have downloaded?

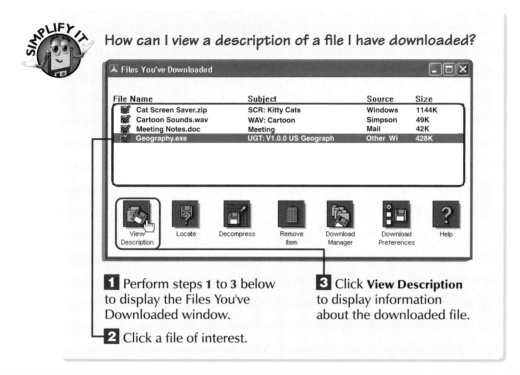

1 Perform steps **1** to **3** below to display the Files You've Downloaded window.

2 Click a file of interest.

3 Click **View Description** to display information about the downloaded file.

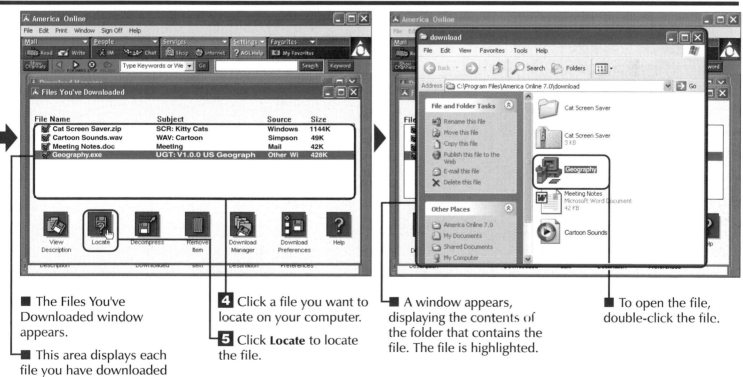

■ The Files You've Downloaded window appears.

■ This area displays each file you have downloaded and information about each file.

Note: If a file was attached to an e-mail message, the Source column displays the word "Mail."

4 Click a file you want to locate on your computer.

5 Click **Locate** to locate the file.

■ A window appears, displaying the contents of the folder that contains the file. The file is highlighted.

■ To open the file, double-click the file.

The filing cabinet stores and organizes information you have gathered on AOL.

You can view the information in the filing cabinet when you are not connected to AOL.

USING THE FILING CABINET

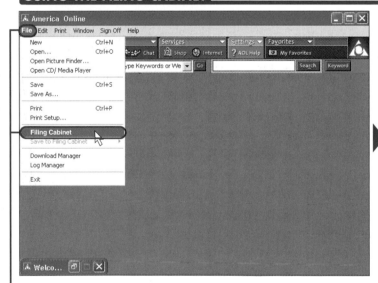

1 Click **File**.

2 Click **Filing Cabinet**.

■ The Filing Cabinet window appears.

3 Click the tab for the information you want to view.

Mail
Stores e-mail messages you have saved and messages waiting to be sent.

Newsgroups
Stores discussion group messages you have chosen to read offline and messages waiting to be sent.

Downloads
Stores files waiting to be downloaded and files you have downloaded.

Can I delete an item from the filing cabinet?

Yes. Deleting items you do not need from the filing cabinet can help reduce clutter in the filing cabinet.

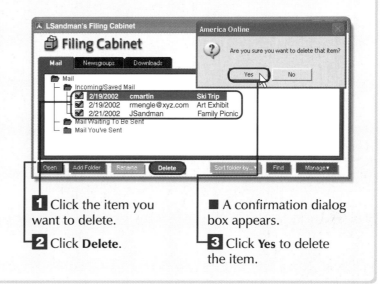

1 Click the item you want to delete.

2 Click **Delete**.

■ A confirmation dialog box appears.

3 Click **Yes** to delete the item.

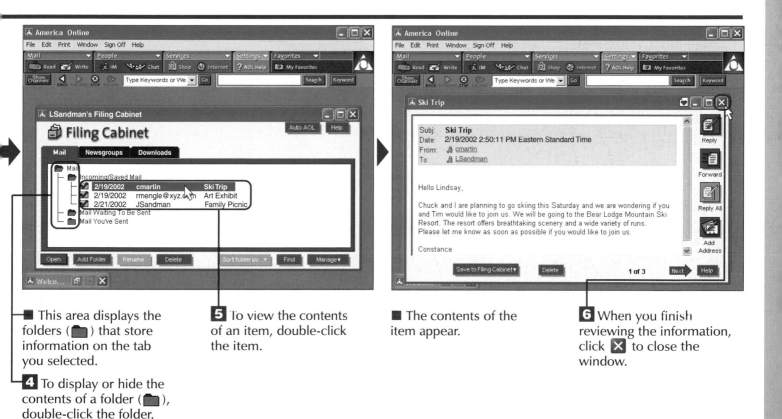

■ This area displays the folders (📁) that store information on the tab you selected.

4 To display or hide the contents of a folder (📁), double-click the folder.

5 To view the contents of an item, double-click the item.

■ The contents of the item appear.

6 When you finish reviewing the information, click ✖ to close the window.

You can take a roll of film to a participating "You've Got Pictures" photo developer to have copies of your developed pictures delivered online to your AOL account.

At the photo developer, you will need to check the AOL box on the order form and provide your AOL screen name. Within a few days, the photo developer will develop your film, scan the pictures and send the pictures to your AOL account.

You do not need a special camera to use this feature.

VIEW NEWLY DEVELOPED PICTURES

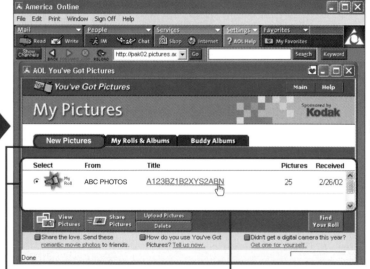

■ If your pictures are ready, the You've Got Pictures icon 🕭 may change to 🕭 and you will hear "You've Got Pictures."

■ If the Welcome window is not displayed, click this area and type **welcome**. Then press the `Enter` key.

1 Click **You've Got Pictures** to display your pictures.

■ The AOL You've Got Pictures window appears.

2 Click the **New Pictures** tab.

■ This area displays your rolls of pictures and information about each roll. A roll of pictures displays the 🌟 symbol.

3 To view the pictures on a roll, click the name of the roll.

■ You may need to use the scroll bar to view the names of all the rolls.

208

SIMPLIFY IT

Where can I find a list of "You've Got Pictures" photo developers?

You can use the keyword **photo developers** to find a participating "You've Got Pictures" photo developer in your area. For information about using keywords, see page 24.

SIMPLIFY IT

My roll of pictures is not displayed in the AOL You've Got Pictures window. What can I do?

You can click the **Find Your Roll** button in the AOL You've Got Pictures window to display the Find Your Roll screen. The Find Your Roll screen displays areas where you can enter the Roll ID and Owner's Key for your pictures. You can find the Roll ID and Owner's Key on the claim card that was included in the envelope when you picked up your pictures. When you finish entering the information, click **Done** to locate your pictures.

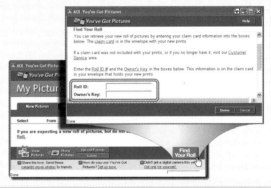

- This area displays a small version of each picture on the roll.

- You may need to use the scroll bar to browse through the pictures.

4 To view a larger version of a picture on the roll, click the picture.

- A larger version of the picture appears.

5 To browse through the large versions of the pictures on the roll, click **Previous Picture** or **Next Picture**.

- To once again display a small version of each picture on the roll, click **View All**.

6 When you finish viewing the pictures on the roll, click ✕ to close the window.

CONTINUED

VIEW YOUR DEVELOPED PICTURES ONLINE

You can redisplay a developed roll of pictures you have previously viewed online.

REDISPLAY DEVELOPED PICTURES

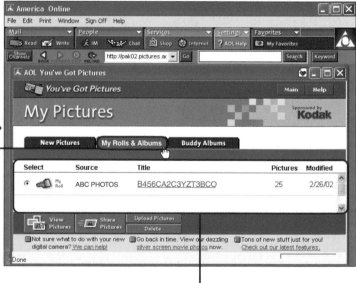

1 Click this area and type **Pictures**. Then press the Enter key.

■ The AOL You've Got Pictures window appears.

2 Click **Go To My Pictures**.

Note: If this screen does not appear, skip to step 3.

■ The My Pictures area appears.

3 Click the **My Rolls & Albums** tab.

■ This area displays the rolls of pictures you have previously viewed and information about each roll. A roll of pictures displays the 📷 symbol.

Can I purchase gifts that display my favorite pictures?

You can purchase extra prints and personalized gifts that display your favorite pictures for your friends and family members. You can buy mugs, jigsaw puzzles, mouse pads, T-shirts and sweatshirts that display your favorite pictures. You will require a credit card number to make any purchases online.

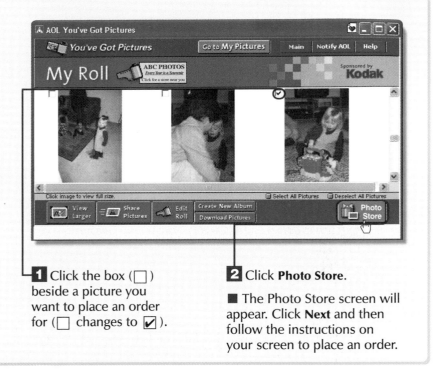

1 Click the box (☐) beside a picture you want to place an order for (☐ changes to ☑).

2 Click **Photo Store**.

■ The Photo Store screen will appear. Click **Next** and then follow the instructions on your screen to place an order.

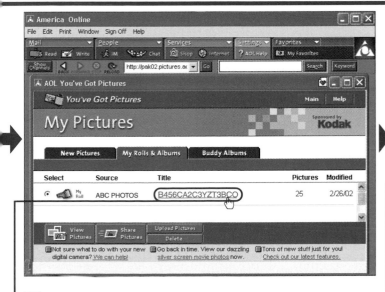

4 To view the pictures on a roll, click the name of the roll.

■ You may need to use the scroll bar to view the names of all the rolls.

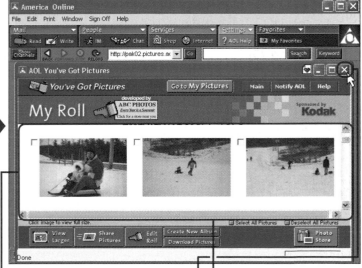

■ This area displays a small version of each picture on the roll.

■ You may need to use the scroll bar to browse through the pictures.

■ To view a larger version of a picture on the roll, you can click the picture.

5 When you finish viewing the pictures on the roll, click ☒ to close the window.

UPLOAD PICTURES TO AOL

After taking pictures with a digital camera or scanning pictures into your computer using a scanner, you can transfer the pictures to an album on AOL. This allows you to share the pictures with friends and family members.

You can consult the documentation that came with your digital camera or scanner to determine how to store pictures from the camera or scanner on your computer.

When you transfer information from your computer to AOL, you are "uploading" the information.

UPLOAD PICTURES TO AOL

1 Click this area and type **Pictures**. Then press the **Enter** key.

■ The AOL You've Got Pictures window appears.

2 Click **Go To My Pictures**.

Note: If this screen does not appear, skip to step 3.

■ The My Pictures area appears.

3 Click **Upload Pictures** to transfer pictures from your computer to AOL.

Why did this screen appear when I tried to upload pictures to AOL?

This screen appears if you have previously uploaded pictures to AOL.

Add Pictures to an Existing Album

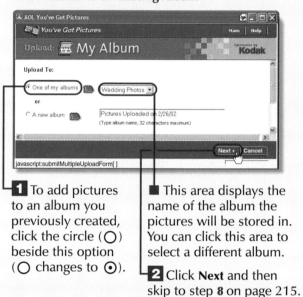

1 To add pictures to an album you previously created, click the circle (○) beside this option (○ changes to ⊙).

■ This area displays the name of the album the pictures will be stored in. You can click this area to select a different album.

2 Click **Next** and then skip to step **8** on page 215.

Add Pictures to a New Album

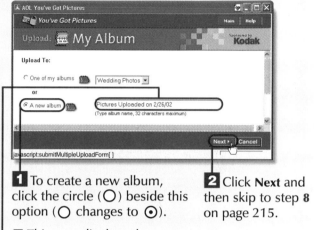

1 To create a new album, click the circle (○) beside this option (○ changes to ⊙).

■ This area displays the name AOL will use for the new album. To use a different name, drag the mouse I over the text and then type a new name.

2 Click **Next** and then skip to step **8** on page 215.

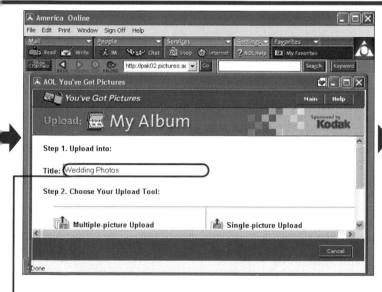

■ AOL stores pictures you upload in an album.

4 This area displays the name of the album AOL will use to store the pictures you upload. To use a different name, type the name.

Note: If a different screen appears, see the top of this page.

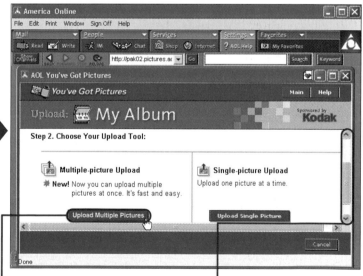

5 Click **Upload Multiple Pictures** to upload pictures to AOL.

■ You may need to use the scroll bar to view the Upload Multiple Pictures button.

CONTINUED

When uploading pictures to AOL, you can select each picture you want to transfer from your computer to AOL.

You can upload a single picture or several pictures at once.

UPLOAD PICTURES TO AOL (CONTINUED)

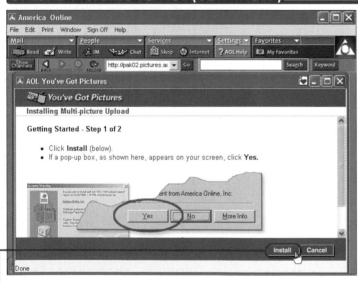

■ Before you can upload pictures for the first time, you must install the Multi-picture Upload tool.

6 Click **Install** to install the Multi-picture Upload tool.

*Note: If this screen does not appear, skip to step **8**.*

■ A warning dialog box may appear. Click **Yes** to continue the installation.

■ This message appears when the Multi-picture Upload tool has been successfully installed.

7 Click **Next** to continue.

How can I quickly select all the pictures in a folder?

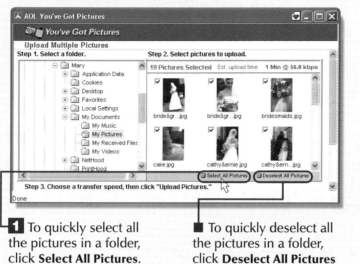

■1 To quickly select all the pictures in a folder, click **Select All Pictures**.

■ All the pictures in the folder are selected (☐ changes to ✓ for each picture).

■ To quickly deselect all the pictures in a folder, click **Deselect All Pictures** (✓ changes to ☐ for each picture).

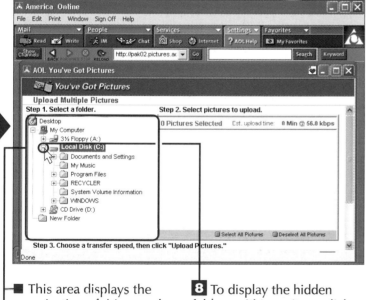

■ This area displays the organization of drives and folders on your computer.

■ An item displaying a plus sign (⊞) contains hidden folders.

■8 To display the hidden folders within an item, click the plus sign (⊞) beside the item (⊞ changes to ⊟).

Note: You can click the minus sign (⊟) beside an item to once again hide the folders within the item (⊟ changes to ⊞).

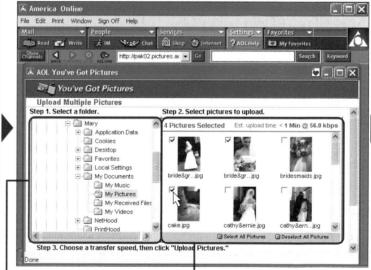

■9 Repeat step 8 until you locate the folder on your computer that contains the pictures you want to upload.

■10 Click the name of the folder that contains the pictures you want to upload.

■ The pictures in the folder appear in this area.

■11 Click the box (☐) beside a picture you want to upload (☐ changes to ✓). Repeat this step for each picture you want to upload.

CONTINUED

You can choose the transfer speed you want to use to upload your pictures to AOL.

The Original Size Upload option takes longer to upload pictures, but uses the best version of each picture you are uploading. The Faster Upload option uploads your pictures more quickly, but uploads lower-quality pictures.

UPLOAD PICTURES TO AOL (CONTINUED)

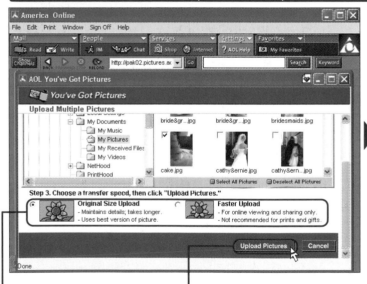

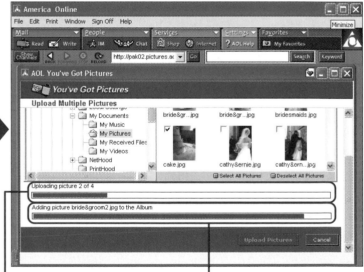

■2 Click the circle (○) beside an option to specify the transfer speed you want to use to upload the pictures (○ changes to ⊙).

■ You may need to use the scroll bar to view the transfer speed options.

■3 Click **Upload Pictures** to upload the pictures you selected.

■ This area displays the progress of the upload.

■ This area displays the progress of the picture that is currently uploading.

How can I later view the pictures I uploaded?

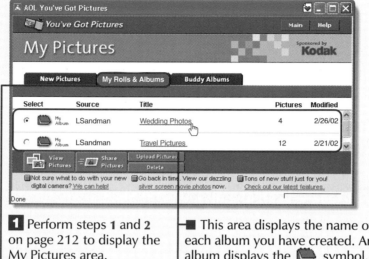

1 Perform steps **1** and **2** on page 212 to display the My Pictures area.

*Note: You may not need to perform step **2** on page 212.*

2 Click the **My Rolls & Albums** tab.

■ This area displays the name of each album you have created. An album displays the 📁 symbol.

3 Click the name of the album you want to view.

■ The album will appear on your screen.

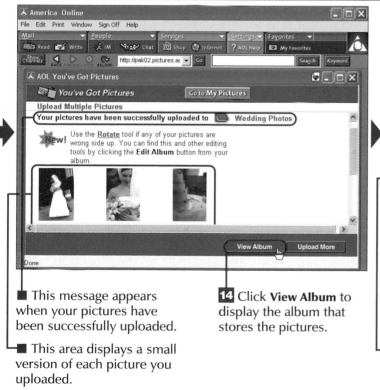

■ This message appears when your pictures have been successfully uploaded.

■ This area displays a small version of each picture you uploaded.

14 Click **View Album** to display the album that stores the pictures.

■ This area displays the name you specified for the album in step **4** on page 213.

■ This area displays the first picture in the album.

15 To browse through the pictures in the album, click **Previous Picture** or **Next Picture**.

16 When you finish viewing the album, click ✕ to close the AOL You've Got Pictures window.

You can share your pictures with friends, family members and colleagues.

You can share your developed pictures and pictures you have uploaded to AOL.

SHARE YOUR PICTURES

1 Click this area and type **Pictures**. Then press the Enter key.

■ The AOL You've Got Pictures window appears.

2 Click **Go To My Pictures**.

Note: If this screen does not appear, skip to step 3.

■ The My Pictures area appears.

3 Click the tab that contains the pictures you want to share.

New Pictures
Contains newly developed rolls of pictures.

My Rolls & Albums
Contains developed rolls of pictures and albums of pictures you have uploaded.

What should I consider when sharing pictures?

You should share only pictures that you have taken yourself or that you have permission to share. When sharing pictures of other people, you should also get permission from the people in the pictures.

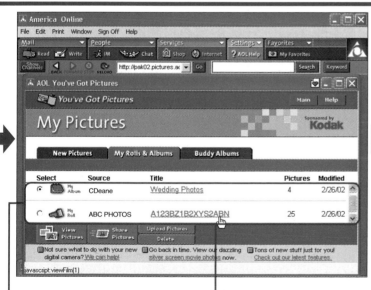

What can people do with the pictures I share with them?

When you share pictures with a person, you send them copies of the pictures. The person will be able to view the pictures, order extra prints and gifts that display the pictures and share the pictures with other people.

■ This area displays the rolls () and albums () on the tab.

■ You may need to use the scroll bar to view all the rolls and albums.

4 Click the roll or album that contains the pictures you want to share.

■ This area displays a small version of each picture on the roll or album.

■ If a large version of a single picture appears, click the **View All** button in the bottom left hand corner of the window to change the view.

5 Click the box (☐) beside a picture you want to share (☐ changes to ☑). Repeat this step for each picture you want to share.

6 Click **Share Pictures**.

CONTINUED

219

SHARE YOUR PICTURES

When sharing pictures, you can specify a name for the Buddy Album AOL will use to send the pictures.

Caribbean Photos

You can share pictures with another AOL member or anyone who has an e-mail address.

SHARE YOUR PICTURES (CONTINUED)

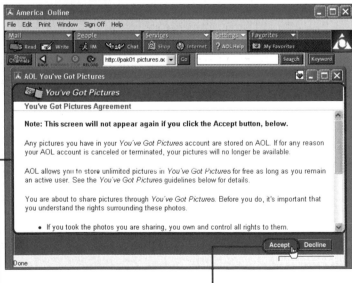

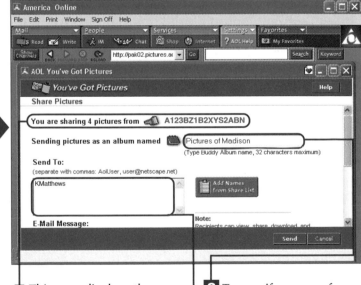

■ The You've Got Pictures agreement appears, displaying information about sharing pictures.

Note: If this screen does not appear, skip to step 8.

7 When you finish reading the agreement, click **Accept** to continue.

■ You may need to use the scroll bar to view the entire agreement.

■ This area displays the number of pictures you selected in step **5** on page 219.

■ AOL will send your pictures in a Buddy Album.

8 To specify a name for the Buddy Album, drag the mouse I over the text in this area and then type the name.

9 Click this area and type the screen name or e-mail address of the person you want to receive the pictures.

How do I view the pictures that another AOL member has shared with me?

When another AOL member shares pictures with you, the pictures appear as a Buddy Album on the New Pictures tab in the My Pictures area.

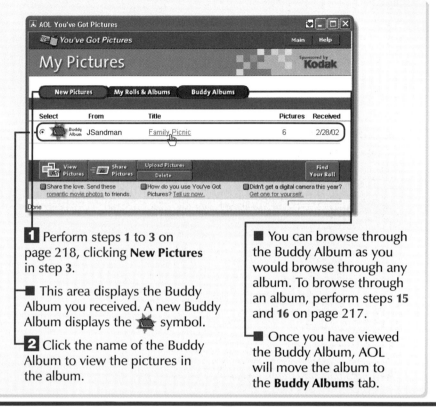

1 Perform steps **1** to **3** on page 218, clicking **New Pictures** in step **3**.

■ This area displays the Buddy Album you received. A new Buddy Album displays the ✹ symbol.

2 Click the name of the Buddy Album to view the pictures in the album.

■ You can browse through the Buddy Album as you would browse through any album. To browse through an album, perform steps **15** and **16** on page 217.

■ Once you have viewed the Buddy Album, AOL will move the album to the **Buddy Albums** tab.

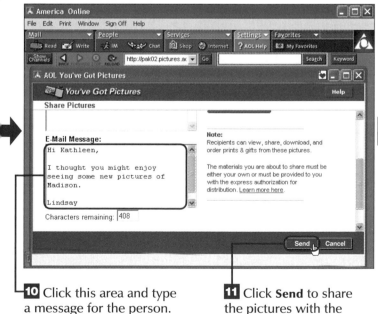

10 Click this area and type a message for the person.

■ You may need to use the scroll bar to view the message area.

11 Click **Send** to share the pictures with the person you specified.

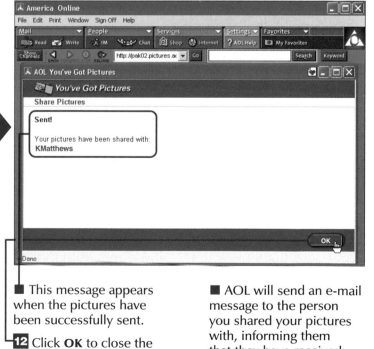

■ This message appears when the pictures have been successfully sent.

12 Click **OK** to close the message.

■ AOL will send an e-mail message to the person you shared your pictures with, informing them that they have received a Buddy Album.

INDEX

Read Less – Learn More™

Visual

with these full-color Visual™ guides

ORDER FORM

TRADE & INDIVIDUAL ORDERS

Phone: **(800) 762-2974**
or **(317) 572-3993**
(8 a.m.–6 p.m., CST, weekdays)
FAX : **(800) 550-2747**
or **(317) 572-4002**

EDUCATIONAL ORDERS & DISCOUNTS

Phone: **(800) 434-2086**
(8:30 a.m.–5:00 p.m., CST, weekdays)
FAX : **(317) 572-4005**

CORPORATE ORDERS FOR VISUAL™ SERIES

Phone: **(800) 469-6616**
(8:30 a.m.–5 p.m., EST, weekdays)
FAX : **(905) 890-9434**

Qty	ISBN	Title	Price	Total

Shipping & Handling Charges

	Description	First book	Each add'l. book	Total
Domestic	Normal	$4.50	$1.50	$
	Two Day Air	$8.50	$2.50	$
	Overnight	$18.00	$3.00	$
International	Surface	$8.00	$8.00	$
	Airmail	$16.00	$16.00	$
	DHL Air	$17.00	$17.00	$

Subtotal _____

*CA residents add
applicable sales tax* _____

*IN, MA and MD
residents add
5% sales tax* _____

*IL residents add
6.25% sales tax* _____

*RI residents add
7% sales tax* _____

*TX residents add
8.25% sales tax* _____

Shipping _____

Total _____

Ship to:

Name _____

Address _____

Company _____

City/State/Zip _____

Daytime Phone _____

Payment: □ Check to Hungry Minds (US Funds Only)
□ Visa □ Mastercard □ American Express

Card # _____ Exp. _____ Signature _____

Hungry Minds™

maranGraphics®